THE MUSÉE D'ORSAY

Coordination Anne Distel and Marc Bascou for this edition.

Texts by : Valérie Bajou, Marc Bascou, Françoise Cachin, Laurence des Cars, Anne Distel, Claire Frèches, Françoise Heilbrun, Geneviève Lacambre, Antoinette Le Normand-Romain, Henri Loyrette, Laure de Margerie, Philippe Néagu, Sylvie Patin, Anne Pingeot, Philippe Thiébaut, Georges Vigne.

I.S.B.N. : 2-7118-3282-1
© Réunion des musées nationaux, 1995.
49 rue Etienne Marcel, 75001 Paris.

The Musée d'Orsay

Contents

Introduction

Antonin Mercié
David, 1872 (détail).

Bronze.
H. 184 ; W. 76.8 ; D. 83.2.
Commissioned in 1872,
acquired in 1874.
*Partial view in front of the
western glass wall and clock of
the former train station.*

The Musée d'Orsay did not automatically win universal recognition. When it first opened in December 1986, reactions to the new museum varied widely–but none were neutral. The interior renovation of the former Orsay railway station by the architectural firm ACT and Gae Aulenti was alternately praised and attacked, as were the curatorial decisions made by Michel Laclotte's team of curators. Many people did not initially realize that a deliberate challenge was being made to the old dualistic view of nineteenth-century art that conveniently divided the second half of the century into, on the one hand, Impressionists and Post-impressionists (who prefigured all of modern art) and, on the other hand, academic hacks who produced official art; the museum was therefore accused of simply exhuming works from Louvre storerooms and culling academic paintings from provincial museums. An opposing criticism argued that the museum did not devote *enough* space to academic works, complaining that the few sunlit exhibition rooms were reserved exclusively for Impressionist canvases. Meanwhile, although some commentators missed the intimacy of the former museum in the Jeu de Paume, most stressed the novelty of a museum able to present all the arts from 1848 to 1914. Indeed, this interdisciplinary approach constituted Orsay's real novelty. Because it focused on a limited time-period–just over half a century–the Musée d'Orsay innovated by displaying not only painting and sculpture (profiting from the fine space of the central alley, or 'nave'), but also the decorative arts, photography, and architecture, not forgetting temporary

Main concourse of Orsay station in 1900.

exhibitions on literature, cinema, music, graphic arts, theatre, etc. The half century in question was an incredibly rich one, ranging from the emergence of Courbet and Millet at the Salons of 1849 and 1850 to the radical break of Picasso's *Demoiselles d'Avignon* (1907), from the building of Paxton's Crystal Palace (1850–1851) to the final accomplishments of Art Nouveau. The museum's exhibitions, lectures, courses and concerts have amply presented this wealth of material, attracting not only a vast "general public" but also thousands of regular visitors who eagerly attend most of Orsay's special events.

The museum's bold decision to move into a former train station is certainly another reason for its success. Once again Orsay paved the way, being the first of many to occupy renovated buildings. Here, visitors physically stroll through a lesson in history and architecture that highlights two prime features of the nineteenth century: historicism (the studied revival of historical styles) and industrial might. Within this complex building–originally inaugurated in 1900 as a vast

The Hotel du Palais d'Orsay in 1900.

Orsay station under construction. Perspective view of girders, entrance hall.

Gabriel Ferrier
L'automne (Autumn), 1900.

Oil on plaster-backed canvas.
Diam. 345.
Détail of dining-room ceiling,
Hotel du Palais d'Orsay.

Benjamin-Constant
*Les routes de l'air (Sky
Paths)*, 1900.

Oil on plaster-backed canvas.
H. 400 ; W. 500.
Ceiling of the reading room,
Hotel du Palais d'Orsay.

Partial view of the reception room, Hotel du Palais d'Orsay.

metallic concourse disguised by facades of stone–spaces had to be created for displaying artworks and convenient passages had to be created for visitors, all the while preserving the identity of the historic building, which served as both station and hotel. This challenge was successfully met by the winners of the 1979 design contest, the architectural firm ACT (architects R. Bardon, P. Colboc, J.P. Philippon), joined in 1980 by Italian architect Gae Aulenti, who won a second competition on interior design and museum layout. Rooms for exhibiting paintings were built along both sides of the nave, capped by terraces. At the top of the building, under the eaves of station and hotel, large galleries devoted to Impressionism were installed to take advantage of daylight. The ballroom and restaurant of the former hotel were carefully restored and incorporated into the museum. The architects decided to eschew neo-1900 pastiche, clearly distinguishing new additions from the original edifice; the railway station's cast-iron piers and beams, as well as its stucco decoration, were thus brought into play, while new structures were designed to enhance the presence of the original building.

The Upper Gallery
Paintings and sculptures by Degas.

The station-museum has now reached cruising speed—a rather lively speed at that, accommodating over twenty-five million visitors. Orsay remains unique, for the initial project has not only retained its novelty and relevance, but has also fulfilled a basic need clearly felt by both French and foreign publics. The museum's staff has evolved (notably with the departure of Françoise Cachin, director from 1986 to 1994), and continues to respond to this need; several modifications have been made in response to certain initial criticisms and in an effort to allow the display of artworks to evolve (fortunately made necessary by new acquisitions). Thus strict chronology has been amended in favor of a more monographic approach: in the Upper Gallery that now commences with the Moreau-Nélation collection and Manet's *Déjeuner sur l'herbe*, the 'New Painting' section henceforth boasts rooms devoted exclusively to Monet, Renoir, Cézanne and, further along, Van Gogh and Gauguin, concluding with a magnificent room of Bonnards. Meanwhile, the 'Pavillon Amont' (Upstream—or eastern—Pavilion) is entirely devoted to architecture and the decorative arts from the France of Viollet-le-Duc to the Britain of Pugin and Mackintosh via turn-of-the-century Vienna. Temporary exhibitions, formerly sprinkled throughout the main circuit, are now grouped into the 'Dossier' rooms on the middle level.

The Upper Gallery, Impressionist paintings.

But the need for regular evolution in display stems above all from the considerable growth of the collections. Even while the museum was being built, works scattered throughout France were being consolidated, and new collections were assembled in the spheres of decorative art, photography, drawing and architecture. Specific purchases were made in order to fill major gaps, notably in the foreign sector. These efforts have been pursued in every field: notable acquisitions include not only Daubigny's *La neige* (Snow), Monet's *Déjeuner sur l'herbe* (Luncheon on the Grass) and *Rue Montorgueil*, Seurat's *Noeud noir* (Black Bow), and Blanche's portrait of *Marcel Proust*, but also objets d'art and furnishings like Gallé's crystal *Hand with Seaweed and Shells*, Van de Velde's oak desk and chair, and Koloman Moser's music case, not to mention canvases by Breiner, Mondrian and Thoma, sculpture by Von Stuck and Klinger, many works by the Nabis, photographs by Degas, and so on.

These new acquisitions—along with the various temporary exhibitions, concerts, film festivals and lecture series—draw many visitors to the museum time and time again. Similarly, this album is designed not only to attest to the wealth of Orsay's collections and to serve as souvenir, but also—and above all—to spark a desire to return to the museum yet again and again.

Henri Loyrette

1

James Pradier

Sapho (Sappho), 1852.

Marble. H. 118 ; W. 70 ; D. 120.
Purchased in 1852.

2

3

Sculpture:
The last Romantics

2
François Rude
Napoléon s'éveillant à l'immortalité (Napoleon Awakening to Immortality), 1846.
Plaster.
H. 215 ; W. 195 ; D. 96.
Purchased in 1891.
The bronze cast is in Fixin, Burgundy.

3
Auguste Préault
Ophélie (Ophelia), Plaster executed in 1842.
H. 75 ; W. 200 ; D. 20.
Purchased and cast in bronze in 1876.

Although Romanticism began to influence painting in the 1820s, it was not until ten years later that the first Romantic sculptures appeared.

Taking their inspiration from Dante, Shakespeare or Chateaubriand, rather than from ancient history, they were intended to be both faithful copies of nature and eloquent expressions of feeling. Antoine Préault (1809-79) exaggerated forms, proportions and modelling. 'Shout louder' was François Rude's exhortation to his wife as she posed for his *Génie de la Patrie (Spirit of Patriotism)* - which was immediately christened 'the shrew in a rage'. Bitterly attacked by the academic critics, these artists found themselves gradually excluded from the Salons during the July Monarchy of King Louis-Philippe (1830-48). Without commissions they were hard put to survive, and had no means of bringing themselves to the public's attention except through publications and the press. In 1847, Rude (1784-1855) executed for a certain Captain Noisot a monument symbolizing that officer's affection and loyalty for his Emperor, whom he had served as Commander of the Grenadiers on the island of Elba, but it was not until the Second Empire that the state gave any sign of official approval. Preault's medallions of Dante and Virgil were acquired by Napoleon III in 1853. Jean-Baptiste Carpeaux (1827-75) found himself in serious trouble at the French school in Rome (the Villa Medicis) over his *Ugolin (Ugolino)*, which represented all that the Institut de France in its role as guardian of the classical tradition most deplored; but state commissions were issued to Jean-Bernard Duseigneur (1809-66) in 1867 for a cast of *Roland furieux (Orlando Furioso)* and to Préault for a cast of his *Ophelie (Ophelia)* in 1876. It should however be noted that the plaster casts of these works dated from 1831 and 1842 respectively !

'I stand not for the finite, but for the infinite' was Preault's inscription on his medallion of Delacroix, now in the Louvre. It is a phrase that neatly encapsulates the spirit of the times, which was to find its fullest expression in the Symbolism of Auguste Rodin who, noted Camille Mauclair, was loved by the poets of his day 'because he makes the most finite of the arts suggest infinity'.

4

5

4
David d'Angers (Pierre-Jean David)
Johann Wolfgang von Goethe (1749-1832).

Plaster. H. 83 ; W. 58 ; D. 51. Permanent loan from the Musée de Saumur. Based on a model executed in Weimar in 1829.

5
Antoine-Louis Barye
La Force (Strength), 1855.

Tinted plaster. H. 100 ; W. 81 ; D. 65. Gift of J. Zoubaloff in 1912. One-third scale model for the exterior of the Denon Pavilion at the new Louvre.

6
Antoine-Louis Barye
La Guerre (War), 1855.

Tinted plaster. H. 105 ; W. 62 ; D. 91. Gift of J. Zoubaloff in 1912. One-third scale model for the exterior of the Richelieu Pavilion at the new Louvre.

6

Ingres, Delacroix, Chassériau after 1850

7

Jean Auguste Dominique
Ingres
La Source (The Spring),
begun in Florence circa1820,
completed in Paris in 1856 with
the aid of Paul Balze and
Alexandre Desgoffe.

Oil on canvas. H. 163 ; W. 80.
Comtesse Duchâtel Bequest,
1878.

At the beginning of the Second Empire (1852-70) the artistic scene was dominated by two great figures: Jean-Auguste-Dominique Ingres (1780-1867) and Eugène Delacroix (1798-1863). The former, the champion of classical art, won the Prix de Rome in 1801 and was elected a member of the Institut de France in 1825; the latter, the leading exponent of Romanticism, was obliged to wait until 1857 before finally being admitted to that august body. Both were appointed to the imperial commission responsible for the Paris World Fair of 1855, the only painters on the committee. This was the first such occasion to include an international retrospective of painting; this was housed in a Palais des Beaux-Arts, constructed especially on the avenue Montaigne. A vast temporary display of the art of the first fifty years of the century, it gave Ingres and Delacroix the ideal opportunity to show some of their best work. Ingres's *Le Source (The Spring)*, a reworking of an earlier study, was not completed until 1856, and was then exhibited in the artist's studio before being put on show by its new owner, Count Duchatel, in a special room 'surrounded by large plants and aquatic flowers, so that the Nymph of the Spring will look even more like a real person'. This 'adolescent Eve', harking back to an 'incalculable antiquity' according to some observers, was to Gustave Moreau an "academy" (in the antique style) ... executed by a marvellous scholar'. *La Source* is the most famous example of the fashion for smooth-textured painting, practised not only by the pupils of Ingres, such as Hippolyte Flandrin (1809-64) or Amaury-Duval (1808-85), but also by Leon Bénouville (1821-59) and other pupils of François Picot (1786-1868), and by students of Charles Gleyre (1806-74), such as Jean-Louis Gérôme (1824-1904). The latter, at the age of only twenty-two, painted a picture which attracted attention at the 1847 Salon and became famous under the title of *Un Combat de coqs (A Cockfight)*, a free interpretation of a classical theme.

Delacroix's technique could hardly have provided a greater contrast. It was much admired by Charles Baudelaire, who called it 'a veritable explosion of colour'. This description of the ambitious canvas *La chasse aux lions (The Lion Hunt)*, commissioned for the Musée de Bordeaux and exhibited in 1855, applies even more aptly to the large, impassioned sketch for it in the Musée d'Orsay, referred to in Delacroix's diary for 3 May 1854: 'In the morning, fired with enthusiasm, went on with the sketch for *The Lion Hunt*.' Featured in all the Delacroix retrospectives, including the posthumous exhibition of 1874, this sketch must inevitably have bad an influence on painters like Manet, Renoir, Signac and Matisse.

In his lifetime, too, Delacroix had his adherents, among than Théodore Chassériau (1819-56), formerly a pupil of Ingres. He was a portraitist and also a painter of goddesses and nymphs,

8

8
Eugène Delacroix
La Chasse aux lions (The Lion Hunt), 1854, Sketch for the painting commissioned by the Musée de Bordeaux and shown at the Paris World Fair of 1855.

Oil on canvas. H. 86 ; W. 115.
Purchased in 1984.

9

9
Théodore Chassériau
*Le Tepidarium ; salle où
les femmes de Pompéi
venaient se reposer et se
sécher en sortant du bain
(Tépidarium: Room
where the Women of
Pompeii Rested and Dried
Themselves on Leaving the
Bath)*, 1853.

Oil on canvas. H. 171 ; W. 258.
Purchased in 1853.

10

11

12

biblical and oriental scenes, and decorative works for churches and public buildings. In the course of his brief career - he was only thirty-seven when he died - he won praise from critics and public alike, because he seemed to bring together 'the two rival schools of drawing and of colour'. *The Tépidarium*, acclaimed at the Salon of 1853, is a case in point: the setting is carefully modelled on Pompeian antiquity, but Chassériau brings his women to life, their languorous poses reminiscent of Delacroix's exotic harem scenes. The half-size figures place Chassériau outside the monumentalist traditions of history painting. *The Tépidarium* was in fact one of the first examples of the historical genre painting which achieved dominance under the Second Empire.

Although the tour of the Musée d'Orsay opens with a tribute to Ingres and Delacroix, showing how their late paintings relate to the works of subsequent painters, it is perhaps worth reiterating that - like Corot, who is also represented in the Musée d'Orsay - they were born in the eighteenth century: the main body of their work remains in the Louvre.

10
Amaury-Duval
*Madame de Loynes
(1837-1908),* 1862.
Oil on canvas. H. 100 ; W. 83.
Jules Lemaitre Bequest, 1914.

11
Jean-Léon Gérôme
Jeunes Grecs faisant battre des coqs, dit *Un combat de coqs (Young Greeks Holding a Cock Fight),*
1846.
Oil on canvas. H. 143 ; W. 204.
Purchased in 1853.

12
Léon Bénouville
Saint François d'Assise, transporté mourant à Sainte-Marie-des-Anges, bénit la ville d'Assise (1226) (The Dying Saint Francis Blessing the City of Assisi, 1226), 1853.
Oil on canvas. H. 93 ; W. 240.
Purchased in 1853.

13
Eugène Guillaume
Le Faucheur (The Reaper),
1849-1855.

Bronze. H. 168 ; W. 78 ; D. 95.
Purchased in 1855.

14
Jules Cavelier
*Cornélie, mère des
Gracques (Cornelia,
Mother of the Gracchi),*
1861.

Marble. H.171 ; W. 121 ; D. 127.
Purchased in 1861.

15
Gabriel-Jules Thomas
Virgile (Virgil), 1859-1861.
Marble. H. 183 ; W. 72 ; p. 56.
Commissioned in 1859, acquired
in 1874.

14

15

Daumier

17

18

19

20

Although during his lifetime Honoré Daumier (1808-79) was renowned chiefly for his caricatures and lithographs, the twentieth-century public is equally appreciative of the paintings and sculptures that he often used as points of departure. The Musée d'Orsay is fortunate in possessing virtually all Daumier's major sculptures. The *Emigrants* and *Ratapoil* have long been in the state collections, and thanks to the generosity of Monsieur Michel David-Weill, these were joined in 1980 by the original series of thirty-six painted clay busts of *Parlementaires (Parliamentarians)*. Begun in 1832, these caricature-portraits of prominent political figures show how Daumier made use of the general vogue for caricature and turned it into a political weapon. He did not rely on anecdote but on piercingly exact observation and wonderfully expressive draughtsmanship and modelling. His bold distortions seem to reveal the inner nature of his subjects, at the same time distinguishing them as clearly identifiable human types. It is this very modern aspect of his work that sets him apart from the Romantics of his generation and justifies the decision to show his sculpture at the Musée d'Orsay rather than in the Louvre.

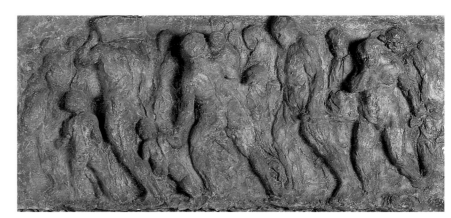

16
Honoré Daumier
La Blanchisseuse (The Washerwoman), circa 1861-1863.

Oil on wood. H. 49 ; W. 33.5.
Purchased with the aid of
D. David-Weill, 1927.

17 to 20
Honoré Daumier
D C. Prunelle (1774-1863)*,
parliamentarian.
H. 31.4 W. 15.2 ; D.15.9 (fig. 17)
C. Philipon (1800-1862),
journalist.
H. 16.4 ; W. 13 ; D. 10.6 (fig. 18)
J.-C. Fulchiron (1774-1859),
poet and parliamentarian.
H. 17.3 ; W. 12.9 ; D. 11.8 (fig. 19)
F. Guizot (1787-1874),
minister of the interior.
H. 22.5 ; W. 17.5 ; D. 15.4 (fig. 20).

21

Colored unfired clay. Purchased
in 1980 with the aid of Michel
David-Weill and the Lutèce
Foundation.
Commissioned by Philipon as
models for lithographs published
1832-35 in his periodicals Le
Charivari and La Caricature.

21
Honoré Daumier
Les Emigrants (The Emigrants), first version,
circa 1848-1850.

Plaster. H. 28 ; W. 66.
Purchased in 1960.

22
Jean-François Millet
Les Glaneuses (Gleaners),
1857.

Oil on canvas. H. 83.5 ; W. 111.
Mme Pommery Bequest, 1890.

Millet

The scenes of peasant life that made Jean-François Millet (1814-75) famous in the 1880s were regarded in his lifetime as subversive. Under the Second Empire not a single one of his canvases was acquired for the Musée du Luxembourg, although two paintings were purchased shortly after Millet's - death *L'église de Gréville (The Church at Gréville)* and a small early picture of *Baigneuses (Bathers)*. However, largely thanks to the generosity of individual collectors, the Louvre has been able to build up over the years a remarkable collection of his work. His *Le printemps (Spring)* was donated in 1887 by the widow of Frédéric Hartmann, who commissioned from Millet a set of *Four Seasons* - never in fact completed. The canvas is a fine example of the painter's late manner. Beautifully lit and with wonderfully clear colours, it is not so much a landscape as the expression of a dialogue between nature, shaped by man, and man himself, a tiny figure under a menacing sky; the symbolism of the season is reinforced by the choice of a morning setting.

23
Jean-François Millet
L'Angélus (The Angelus),
1857-1859.

Oil on canvas. H. 55.5 ; W. 66.
Alfred Chauchard Bequest, 1909.

23

Millet's characteristic brand of Naturalism consists in this ability to evoke a precise instant while yet investing it with a universal significance. The most famous example of his work is *L'Angélus (The Angelus)*, which came to the Louvre as part of a bequest by Alfred Chauchard in 1909. He acquired it in 1890 from the American Art Association, which had taken the picture on a triumphant tour of the American cities after buying it, only a year before, at the Secretan sale of 1 July 1889.*Des glaneuses (Gleaners)* passed to the Louvre in 1890. This major work had attracted bitter criticism when first exhibited at the Salon of 1857. In an age when it was believed that poverty had been eradicated, the painting seemed to conjure up the spectre of revolution. Paul de Saint-Victor wrote in *La Presse*: 'While Monsieur Courbet is tidying up and adjusting his style, Monsieur Millet is becoming more entrenched in his. His three *Gleaners* have immoderate pretensions; they pose like the Three Fates of Pauperism. They are scarecrows in rags.' Millet's cause was, however, taken up by one critic, Jules Castagnary, who sensed the emergence of a new style that would replace the exhausted genre of history painting. Castagnary chose therefore to find a parallel with the classical past, describing the canvas as 'one of the great and true passages such as Homer and Virgil lighted upon'. The comparison is not inapt: the gleaners recall the sculptures of the Parthenon. Their massive weight is an essential part of their power of expression.

24
Jean-François Millet
Le Printemps (Spring),
1868-1873.

Oil on canvas. H. 86 ; W. 111.1.
Gift of Mme Frédéric Hartmann,
1887.

24

The Barbizon School; late Corot

25

Théodore Rousseau
Une avenue, forêt de L'Isle-Adam (A Lane in L'Isle-Adam Forest), 1849.

Oil on canvas. H. 101 ; W. 82.
Alfred Chauchard Bequest, 1909.

26

Narcisse Diaz de la Peña
Les Hauteurs du Jean de Paris (forêt de Fontainebleau)
(Jean de Paris Heights, Forest of Fontainebleau), 1867.

Oil on canvas. H. 84 ; W. 106.
Alfred Chauchard Bequest, 1909.

Millet went to live at Barbizon in 1849, and continued to paint scenes of peasant life, looking to the village itself or the Chailly plain for his subject matter rather than the nearby forest of Fontainebleau itself. That great area of woodland had for some twenty years been a favourite spot for artists, who arrived in their numbers to paint and draw from nature. One of these was Millet's friend Théodore Rousseau (1812-67), who had suffered many rejections at the hands of the academic jury under Louis-Philippe, and began to receive official recognition only after 1848, in the Second Republic. A perfectionist, he reworked his paintings obsessively and made it a rule to paint always from the motif - as for example in the forest landscape pierced by a vertical shaft of sunlight, exhibited at the Salon of 1849 as *Une avenue (An avenue)*, which he painted in the spring of 1846 while staying with the landscapist Jules Dupré at L'Isle-Adam.

Narcisse Diaz de la Peña (1807-76) started out as a painter of amorous interludes and fantasies in a Romantic spirit, and by 1860 was successful enough to enjoy an extravagant lifestyle. After meeting Théodore Rousseau in 1837, he returned regularly to Fontainebleau and became perhaps the most skilled of all the group at conveying the effects of light on the trees and undergrowth. The critic Thoré noted that Diaz's supremacy lay in 'the quality of the colour, which is always determined by the light', and that 'his pictures resemble a mound of precious

25

26

27
Jean-Baptiste Camille Corot
*L'Atelier de Corot. Jeune
femme pensive une mando-
line à la main (Corot's
Studio. Young Woman with
Mandolin),* circa 1865.

Oil on canvas. H. 56 ; W. 46.
Purchased in 1933.

28
Jean-Baptiste Camille Corot
*Une matinée. La danse des
nymphes (Morning. The
Dance of the Nymphs),*
1850-1851.

Oil on canvas. H. 98 ; W. 131.
Purchased in 1851.

stones'. His technique almost certainly influenced Monticelli and Renoir, to whom he gave advice and encouragement.

Rousseau and Diaz have close ties with Romanticism and, like Delacroix, are represented in the Musée d'Orsay only by a few works of particular significance (notably those from the Chauchard collection; see p. 65). The rest of their work is to be seen in the Louvre.

Another major painter whose works are mainly in the Louvre, but who is represented in the Musée d'Orsay collections, is Jean-Baptiste Camille Corot (1796-1875), born in the eighteenth century but active well into the nineteenth. His career was unsensational, but he was greatly esteemed by the younger painters and by the more perspicacious of the critics, among them Charles Baudelaire who admired his technique and 'unfailingly strict harmonies'.

Corot travelled in Italy, stayed at Barbizon. and ranged the length and breadth of France, from Brittany to Dauphiné. To make his work acceptable to the academic Salon jury, he felt obliged to introduce historical and mythological figures into landscapes that otherwise would have been rejected as little more than sketches. It was the increasing respectability of Naturalism in the Second Empire that presented him with the freedom to pursue his own inclinations, encouraged too, no doubt, by the expansion in demand from private patrons.

28

At about this time his manner became more lyrical and he began to paint misty evocations of nature (well represented in the Chauchard collection). *La danse des nymphes (The Dance of the Nymphs)* is typical; it was exhibited at the Salon of 1850-51 and purchased by the state for the Musée du Luxembourg, where it was put on show in 1854 - the only painting by Corot to be given that official stamp of approval during his lifetime.

Less well-known, and largely dismissed by his contemporaries, is Corot's painting of individual figures, posed either outdoors or in studio interiors, and dressed in exotic disguises or theatrical costumes. Corot treated these works as exercises in pure painting, anticipating Cezanne's fundamental explorations of technique. Although he also painted portraits of friends and relatives, for studies of this type Corot preferred to employ professional models, not wishing to be distracted by individual personality. The melancholy of the attitude of the pensive young woman in *L'atelier (The Studio)* is tempered by the play of light on her dress and face, and on the tapestry of the chair to the left; there is a discreet symbolism in the objects about her, the landscape on the easel making a reference to painting and the mandolin suggesting a tune left unfinished.

29
Antoine Chintreuil
L'Espace (Space), 1869.
Oil on canvas.
Purchased in 1869.

Daubigny
Meissonier

Charles-François Daubigny (1817-78) belonged to the generation of Millet and Courbet. Both engraver and painter, he had a traditional education and went to Italy before devoting himself to observation of the French landscape. By 1848 his success was established, and as a member of the Salon jury under the Second Empire he was able to put in a word for younger artists such as Cézanne, Renoir and Pissarro. He worked all over France, and in 1860 was among the first of many painters to move to Auvers-sur-Oise, where his visitors included Daumier and Corot. Daubigny loved effects of light on water, and sailed the rivers of the Ile-de-France in his studio-boat *Botin*. The handling and bold touches of *La neige (Snow)*, playing on black and white, reveal Daubigny's contact with the younger generation. Antoine Chintreuil (1814-73) was much influenced by Corot and regarded himself as his pupil. He acquired some reputation under the Second Republic, showing at the juryless Salon of 1848, but in 1863 was relegated to the Salon des Refusés. His fame was largely posthumous, although at the 1869 Salon *L'espace (Space)*, a delicate composition of greens and blues, was praised for 'a fine appreciation of light' and bought for the Luxembourg. On a completely different register, an artist like Ernest Meissonier (1815-91) remained

30

31
Ernest Meissonier
*Campagne de France, 1814
(The 1814 Campaign in
France)*, 1864.

Oil on wood. H. 51.5 ; W. 76.5.
Alfred Chauchard Bequest, 1909.

32

faithful to the idea of carefully-observed realism, dressing his models in authentic costume and exhaustively researching every aspect of period detail. His genre pictures, often minute in size, attracted high prices from collectors, and many are in the fine collection assembled at the end of the nineteenth century by Alfred Chauchard and bequeathed by him to the Louvre in 1909. A project that occupied Meissonier throughout most of his career was a series of five paintings in commemoration of the epic career of Napoleon. One of these is *Campagne de France 1814 (The Campaign in France, 1814)*, which was exhibited at the Salon of 1864. Together with Millet's *Angelus*, this is one of the gems of the Chauchard Collection, in which sumptuously framed landscapes and Naturalist scenes are mingled with tiny genre paintings, among which, interestingly, are a few Romantic works such as *Marchand turc fumant dans sa boutique (Turkish Merchant Smoking in his Shop)* by Alexandre Decamps (1803-60).

32
Alexandre Gabriel Decamps
Marchand turc fumant dans sa boutique (Turkish Merchant Smoking in his Shop), 1844.

Oil on canvas. H. 36 ; W. 28.
Alfred Chauchard Bequest, 1909.

33
Ernest Meissonier
Le Voyageur (The Traveller).

Colored wax and cloth.
H. 47.8 ; W. 60 ; D. 39.5. Gift of Jean Du Pasquier, 1984, in memory of his mother, the artist's grand-daughter.

33

Courbet

Gustave Courbet (1819-77) experienced years of struggle in the early part of his career, in the reign of Louis-Philippe: only three of the twenty-four canvases he submitted to the Salon in the period 1841-47 were accepted by the jury and exhibited. The situation changed dramatically when he showed ten canvases at the juryless Salon of 1848 and went on to win a medal in 1849 - which meant that he could in future bypass the jury procedure. His fame was assured, but the critics were divided into two camps at the Salon of 1850-51 by the controversial *Un enterrement à Ornans (Burial at Ornans)*, a vast composition for which Courbet used people from his home town of Ornans as models. When the selection jury for the World Fair of 1855 turned down the work, along with his recent manifesto-painting *L'atelier du peintre (The Painter in his Studio)*, Courbet determined to hold a show of his own in competition with the officially blessed international retrospective - although in fact eleven of his canvases had been included. In the event the Pavillon du Réalisme, with an exhibition of forty of his paintings, was not a success; only his friends praised the venture, among them the critic Champfleury, generous

54

35

enough to overlook the portrait of himself in *The Painter in his Studio*, which he disliked intensely.

Courbet's two major compositions did not enter the national collections until many years later: the *Burial at Ornans* was presented to the Louvre to coincide with an exhibition held at the Ecole des Beaux-Arts in 1882, 'Exposition des oeuvres de G. Courbet', marking the artist's long-delayed official recognition, and the *Studio* remained in private hands until 1920.

Apart from these paintings, which shocked the Second Empire public and were satirized by the cartoonists of the day, Courbet also produced many far more accessible works that appealed to collectors and yet remained honest expressions of his robust style. Count Nieuwerkerke, Director of the Beaux-Arts in the Second Empire, purchased with funds from the Emperor's civil list a landscape called *Le ruisseau couvert (The Shaded Stream)*, painted in 1865, which then passed to the national collections. *La vague (The Wave)* was acquired for the Musée du Luxembourg shortly after the painter's death. *La falaise d'Etretat apres l'orage (The Cliff at Etretat after the Storm)*, of the Salon of 1870, is a fine example of Courbet's qualities as a landscape artist; like *The Wave*, it was painted in 1869, while Courbet was staying at Etretat, a small town on the Normandy coast which had been a favourite spot for painters since the early years of the century.

36

Gustave Courbet
L'Atelier du peintre.
Allégorie réelle détermi-
nant une phase de sept
années de ma vie artistique
(The Studio of the Painter.
A Real Allegory Defining
a Seven-year Phase in my
Artistic Life), exhibited in the
Realism Pavilion, Place de
l'Alma (Paris), in 1855.

Oil on canvas. H. 361 ; W. 598.
Purchased in 1920 thanks to a
public subscription, and to the
Société des Amis du Louvre.

36

Peasant Realism

Jules Breton (1827-1906), educated in Antwerp and Paris, experimented from 1849-50 onwards with large-scale Realist compositions in the style of Courbet or Alexandre Antigna. He later concentrated on studies of agricultural workers in the fields around his native village of Courrières, in Artois (near Calais). His paintings of peasants are more anecdotal than those by Millet, and he won popular acclaim in the Second Empire for such pictures as *Le rappel des glaneuses (Calling the Gleaners Home)*. Regarded practically as the official painter of peasant life, he was elected a member of the Institut de France in 1886, at a time when Naturalism was no longer controversial.

The mid-century pioneers of this agricultural genre were Constant Troyon (1810-65) and Rosa Bonheur (1822-99); Bonheur's *Labourage nivernais, le sombrage (First Ploughing, Nivernais Region)*, commissioned by the state in 1848, has for succeeding generations evoked the world of George Sand's novels.

Ernest Hébert (1817-1908) is in a slightly different category. After winning the Prix de Rome in 1839 he made several trips to Italy, and there abandoned history painting to concentrate instead on scenes of popular life, following the example set by Leopold Robert and Victor Schnetz; his masterpiece, *La Mal'aria (Mal'aria)*, in the Salon of 1850-51, reflected the prevailing Realist vein. His later compositions, however, are tinged with the sentimentality that brought him numerous commissions and great success as a painter of female portraits.

37
Jules Breton
Le Rappel des glaneuses (Calling the Gleaners Home), 1859.
Oil on canvas. H. 90 ; W. 176.
Gift of Napoléon III, 1862.

37

38
Constant Troyon
Garde-chasse arrêté
près de ses chiens
(Gamekeeper Standing
with his Dogs), 1854.

Oil on canvas. H. 117 ; W. 90.
Alfred Chauchard Bequest, 1909.

38

39

39
Rosa Bonheur
Labourage nivernais ;
le sombrage (First
Ploughing, Nivernais
Region), 1849.

Oil on canvas. H. 134 ; W. 260.
National commission, 1848.

40
Ernest Hébert
La Mal'aria (Mal'aria),
1848-1849.

Oil on canvas. H. 135 ; W. 193.
Purchased in 1851.

40

41
Gustave Guillaumet
Le Sahara, dit aussi
Le Désert (The Sahara, or,
The Desert), 1867.

Oil on canvas. H. 110 ; W. 200.
Gift of the artist's family, 1888.

Orientalism

42
Eugène Fromentin
*Chasse au faucon en
Algérie ; la curée (Falconry
in Algeria; Distributing the
Quarry),* 1863.

Oil on canvas. H. 162.5 ; W. 118.
Purchased in 1863.

The Orient, as seen from nineteenth-century France, consisted of the Muslim countries of the Mediterranean, either as they existed in the imagination - for example in Ingres' *Odalisques* - or as they were actually experienced at first hand: the Holy Land and Eastern Turkey, painted by Charles Tournemine (1812-72); Egypt, in the works of Leon Belly (1827-77), among them the impressive *Pélerins allant à la Mecque (Pilgrims Travelling to Mecca)* of the Salon of 1861; and above all North Africa, which Delacroix had described after a visit in 1832 as a place where the ancient civilizations lived on. Apart from the obvious attraction of new subject matter, with its glimpses of a lost Eden, there was also the dazzling quality of the light, which spurred the painters to transform their palettes. The Romanticism of Delacroix, Decamps, Chassériau and, later in the day, Henri Regnault, gave way during the Second Empire to an increasing Naturalism, a trend noted in 1861 by the brothers Jules and Edmond de Goncourt in their novel *Manette Salomon.*

42

Eugene Fromentin (1820-76) visited Algeria on several occasions between 1846 and 1853, and in 1857 and 1859 published two accounts of his travels, *Un été dans le Sahara* and *Une année dans le Sahel*. These trips were to furnish him with subject matter for the rest of his life, and, drawing on his memories, he painted numerous imaginary scenes and picturesque reconstructions such as *Chasse au faucon en Algérie: la curée (Falconry in Algeria: Distributing the Quarry)* acquired for the Musée du Luxembourg at the Salon of 1863, a brilliantly coloured canvas with drawing of an almost Ingres-like perfection. More obviously in the Naturalist spirit is the painting of Gustave Guillaumet (1840-87), who renounced the traditional study period in Rome and went instead to North Africa, making some ten trips in all.

Biblical lands were the object of Naturalist reconstitution in a painting like *Jerusalem* by Jean-Léon Gérôme (1824–1904). This work illustrates how an academic painter attempted to rejuvenate religious art by stressing authenticity and original settings (partly inspired by the 1863 publication of Ernest Renan's influential *Life of Jesus*).

43
Jean-Léon Gérôme
Jerusalem, 1867.
Oil on canvas. H. 82 ; W. 144.
Purchased in 1990.

44
Louis-Ernest Barrias
Fileuse de Mégare (The Spinner of Megara), 1870.
Marble. H. 126 ; W. 63 ; D. 66.
Purchased in 1870.

44

45

46

45
Carolus-Duran
La Dame au gant (Lady with Glove), Mᵐᵉ Carolus-Duran, née Pauline Croizette (1839-1912), painter, 1869.

Oil on canvas. H. 228 ; W. 164. Purchased in 1875.

46
Alfred Stevens
Ce qu'on appelle le vagabondage dit aussi *Les Chasseurs de Vincennes (What People Call Vagrancy,* or *the Hunters of Vincennes),* circa 1854.

Oil on canvas. H. 130 ; W. 165. Bequest of the painter Léon Lhermitte, 1926.

Further aspects of Realism;
Fantin-Latour

Other painters allied themselves with Realism in their choice of modern themes, but retained a meticulous traditional technique. This official Realism, always in the best of taste, is represented by Alfred Stevens (1823-1906), James Tissot (1836-1902) and Carolus-Duran (1838-1910). The modernity of these fashionable painters consisted in an idealized image of an elegant and charming bourgeoisie.

Stevens studied in Brussels under a pupil of Jacques-Louis David and then moved to Paris, where he made his Salon début with paintings on humanitarian themes, such as *Ce qu'on appelle le vagabondage (What People Call Vagrancy)*. The picture is a powerful, frieze-like composition with flattened perspective and simplified forms, but the mood is one of melodramatic pathos. A friend of Manet, Stevens did on occasion paint Naturalist scenes such as *La baignoire (The Bath)*, also in the Musée d'Orsay, but his fame depended on his evocations of the affluent bourgeois world.

Attention to detail in the setting, and meticulous rendering of costumes, characterize the work of Tissot, who started out as a painter of historical genre scenes, represented in the Musée d'Orsay by his sparkling *Faust et Marguerite (Faust and Gretchen)*. Patronized by the rich and famous, Tissot breathed new life into the traditionally static form of the society portrait, a fine example being his portrait of an unknown *Young Woman*, identified as L.L. (1864).

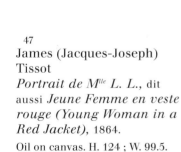

47

47
James (Jacques-Joseph) Tissot
Portrait de Mlle L. L., dit aussi *Jeune Femme en veste rouge (Young Woman in a Red Jacket)*, 1864.
Oil on canvas. H. 124 ; W. 99.5.
Purchased in 1907.

48
Théodule Ribot
Saint Sebastian, Martyr, 1865.
Oil on canvas. H. 97 ; W. 130.
Purchased in 1865.

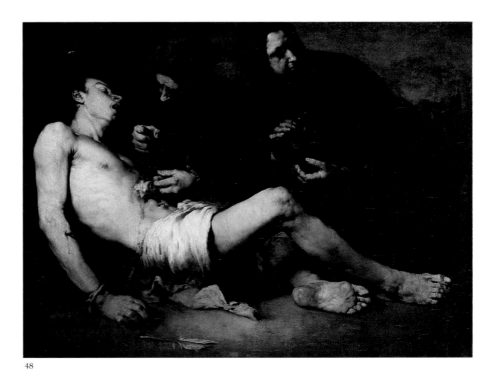

48

La dame au gant (Lady with a Glove) is typical of Carolus-Duran's portraiture; the dark colours and the spirited handling reflect the artist's admiration for Spanish painting. The anecdotal detail of the dropped glove is a reminder that the society portrait is really a genre scene, and that bourgeois Realism is an undemanding option.

Théodule Ribot (1823-91) received a traditional training as a pupil of Auguste Glaize. He specialized mostly in domestic interiors, often introducing everyday objects and members of his family as in *La ravaudeuse (Woman Darning)*, in the Musée d'Orsay. His *Saint Sébastien (St Sebastian)* was acquired for the nation at the Salon of 1865. His predilection for religious subjects sets him apart from the other Realists, although it indicates not so much intensity of feeling as admiration for seventeenth-century Spanish art, and for José Ribera in particular.

Henri Fantin-Latour (1836-1904) studied under Horace Lecoq de Boisbaudran, learning from him the importance of visual memory in drawing. He formed his artistic allegiances as the result of copying paintings in the Louvre, and his first major composition was *Hommage à Delacroix (Homage to Delacroix)*, inspired by the Dutch group-portraits of the seventeenth century. Fantin-Latour was a friend of Manet and the future Impressionists, who appear in *Un atelier aux Batignolles (A Studio in the Batignolles Quarter)*, of 1870. He shared with them

49
Henri Fantin-Latour
Coin de table (Corner Discussion), 1872.

Oil on canvas. H. 160 ; W. 225. Bequeathed in 1911 by M. and Mme Léon-Emile Petitdidier (called Blémont), who enjoyed usufruct until 1920.
Left to right: Verlaine, Rimbaud, E. Bonnier, L. Valade, E. Blémont, J. Aicard, E. d'Hervilly, C. Pelletan.

50
Henri Fantin-Latour
Un Atelier aux Batignolles (A Studio in the Batignolles Quarter), 1870.

Oil on canvas. H. 204 ; W. 273.5. Purchased in 1892.
Left to right: O. Schölderer, Manet, Renoir, Z. Astruc, E. Zola, E. Maitre, Bazille, Monet.

49

50

a taste for modern life and a dislike of anecdotal painting. His *Un Coin de table (Corner of a Table)* of 1872, takes liberties with conventional perspective in order to make the figures of Verlaine and Rimbaud the central feature of the composition. This is the only known portrait of the latter.

In the latter half of his career Fantin-Latour painted numerous still-lifes, which show meticulous observation and an interest in light effects. His rather austere portraits focus all the attention on the face, the simplicity of the presentation emphasising the character of the sitter. But the paintings in which he took the greatest pleasure were poetic compositions, transpositions into visual terms of his response to literature or to the music of Wagner, Berlioz or Schumann.

Plein air
landscape painting

In the first half of the nineteenth century there were numerous landscape painters who insisted on the need to observe nature faithfully and to set down at speed, working in the open air *(en plein-air)* and with the motif before them, the ephemeral character of the scene that presented itself to their eyes. In England there were, most notably, John Constable, J. M. W. Turner and Richard Bonington, and in France a line from Paul-Henri de Valenciennes through to Corot and the Barbizon School. Their heirs, in the middle years of the century, were J. B. Jongkind and Eugene Boudin, who developed these principles in the 1850s, each in his own distinctive manner. Jongkind (1819–91) was Dutch but lived and worked in France. He evolved a very free and spirited technique, which, combined with his Realist inclinations, was enough to ensure his presence - alongside Manet - at the Salon des Refusés of 1863; the picture by which he was represented was a landscape, *Ruines du chateau de Rosemont (The Ruined Chateau at Rosemont).* He was a watercolourist of exceptional talent and produced many striking landscapes of Holland, the Ile-de-France, Paris and Montmartre, the Normandy coast and the Isère. The French national museums are fortunate to have in

51
Johan Barthold Jongkind
Ruines du château de Rosemont (Ruined Chateau at Rosemont), 1861.

Oil on canvas. H. 34 ; W. 56.5.
Etienne Moreau-Nélaton Bequest, 1906.

51

52

their possession a superb series of his watercolours, thanks to the generosity of the collector Etienne Moreau-Nélaton.

Eugène Boudin (1824-98) studied for a brief period in Paris and was advised by Isabey and Troyon. Corot and Courbet were the painters whose example he admired, but it was above all his friend Jongkind who influenced him in the course he would follow. Boudin was born in Honfleur and died in Deauville: his painting is rooted in that area of the Normandy coast where he spent so much of his life. Later, when he was famous and could afford to travel, he painted also in Brittany, around Bordeaux, in the South of France, Venice and Holland. It was in 1862 that he began to paint scenes showing the crowds of elegant summer visitors on the beaches of Deauville and Trouville - a theme that verged almost on genre painting. Yet the apparent superficiality of the subject seemed to release his powers of expression. These bright paintings, pulsating with light, were to make a deep impression on the young Claude Monet, whose family lived in Le Havre. 'If I have become a painter, I owe it to Eugene Boudin,' he wrote, underlining the importance of the role Boudin played in the genesis of Impressionism. Monet also knew Jongkind well, and stayed with Bazille at the Ferme Saint-Siméon near Honfleur. This simple farmhouse became famous for the numbers of artists who stayed there in the nineteenth century, among them Diaz, Troyon, Daubigny, Corot and Courbet. There are major works by these painters, sometimes called the Pre-Impressionists, in the Eduardo Mollard collection, which, in accordance with the benefactor's wishes, is kept together in the Musée d'Orsay.

Painting in Lyon and Provence

In the second half of the nineteenth century Paris was the centre of artistic life in France. Nevertheless, there were certain figures of powerful originality, a little apart from the mainstream, who lived and worked in relative isolation in the provinces. They in turn attracted admirers and imitators, and so founded regional schools of painting. The most obvious example is F. A. Ravier (1814-95), who, although initially a pupil of Corot, belongs to the School of Lyon. His free handling of skyscapes reflects the influence of Turner. Another outsider was Adolphe Monticelli (1824–86), who studied in Marseille and continued to work in the South of France even after he became nominally resident in Paris. His admiration for Delacroix and for the virtuosity of Diaz led him to develop a brilliant technique using heavy impasto, which came as a revelation to the young Vincent van Gogh. Also a southerner, Monticelli's friend Paul Guigou (1833-71) was a great admirer of Courbet. He was chiefly interested in the effects produced by the strong sunlight of Provence, and his studies on that theme are somewhat reminiscent of those by his young contemporary Fréderic Bazille.

53

54

53
Paul Guigou
*Lavandière
(Washerwoman),* 1860.
Oil on canvas. H. 81 ; W. 59.
Gift of Paul Rosenberg, 1912.

54
Adolphe Monticelli
*Nature morte au pichet
blanc (Still-life with White
Jug),* circa 1878-1880.
Oil on wood. H. 49 ; W. 63.
Purchased in 1937.

Manet

When Edouard Manet (1832-83), a friend of the notorious poet Baudelaire, sent in to the 1863 Salon jury his *Déjeuner sur l'herbe*, then known as *Le bain (Bathing)*, he was already, in the eyes of the younger artists and critics, a leader of what we would now term the avant-garde (although he had received official approval in 1861 for a daringly free exercise in the 'Spanish vein'). *Le bain* was rejected; and indeed the jury turned down so many paintings that year that Napoleon III himself opened a supplementary Salon. This was the famous Salon des Refuses, and there *Le bain* was an overnight sensation.

The picture was regarded as shocking both because it was painted with the freedom of a sketch and because of its subject - never mind that it was derived from an engraving by Raphael, the very painter most revered by the Ecole des Beaux-Arts. Certainly the subject was provocative: a naked woman posing unconcernedly in the company of two well-dressed young men who looked like students. 'Monsieur Manet seeks to make his name by shocking the bourgeoisie... his taste is corrupted by a love of the bizarre,' wrote a critic of the day, failing to understand what Manet was trying to do - which was to transpose into a modern setting a traditional theme of Renaissance Italy, to create a contemporary version of the 'pastoral interlude' or *concert champêtre*.

An even greater scandal was sparked off by *Olympia* (1863) at the Salon of 1865. Once again Manet had transformed an idealized nude - Titian's *Venus of Urbino* into a provocative and quasi-photographic image that showed a hidden side of life in the Second Empire: a naked prostitute with a challenging gaze, lying on her bed. Today we can still respond to the provoking fascination of this nude, but the 'immorality' of the context has lost its force. The painting is above all an extraordinary *tour de force*, both for its technique and its subject matter, a masterpiece of sensual expression that links the great classical art of the past with modern painting. The female figure who in her own day was seen as a 'redhead of out-and-out ugliness'. a 'yellow-bellied odalisque', a 'Queen of Spades', looks now - because of the handling and the dazzling use of colour, the contradictions and the humour, even because of that brazen stare - like a Mona Lisa of the modern age.

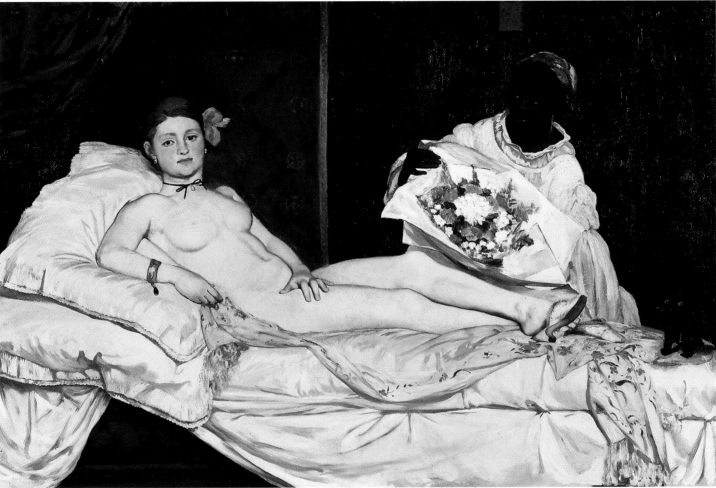

56

55
Edouard Manet
Le Déjeuner sur l'herbe,
1863.

Oil on canvas. H. 208 ; W. 264.5.
Etienne Moreau-Nélaton Bequest,
1906.

56
Edouard Manet
Olympia, 1863.

Oil on canvas. H. 130.5 ; W. 190.
Presented to the nation by a
public subscription launched
by Claude Monet, 1890.

57

58

As a young man Emile Zola was an astute and far-sighted critic. Manet painted his portrait as a gesture of gratitude for the impassioned defence of his work issued by the twenty-eight-year-old writer. In this portrait Zola is surrounded by objects reflecting his tastes and concerns: Japanese prints, engravings by Manet, Naturalist novels and, lying under his pen, the little blue book in which he wrote his defence of Manet. At the next Salon, of 1869, Manet exhibited *Le balcon (The Balcony)*, a contemporary treatment of a theme used by Goya. Seated in the foreground, in front of the painter Antoine Guillemet and the young violinist Fanny Claus, is one of Manet's favourite models, the beautiful Berthe Morisot, soon to join the Impressionist ranks as a painter in her own right.

Spurned by the authorities in the painter's lifetime, Manet's work came to be represented in the state museums only as the result of generous donations by private individuals and friends. In 1890 Claude Monet organized a campaign to purchase *Olympia* for the nation from Manet's widow. *The Balcony* entered the national collections as part of the controversial Gustave Caillebotte bequest, followed by *Le déjeuner sur l'herbe* in the Etienne Moreau-Nélaton gift of 1906. and *Le fifre (The Fifer)* in the collection of Count Isaac de Camondo, left to the state in 1911. These and other gifts and acquisitions have ensured that the museum now possesses an outstanding selection of Manet's works, including some of his finest pastels.

57
Edouard Manet
Emile Zola (writer, 1840-1902), 1868.

Oil on canvas. H. 146.5 ; W. 114. Bequeathed in 1918 by Mme Emile Zola, who enjoyed usufruct until 1925.

58
Edouard Manet
Le Balcon (The Balcony),
Berthe Morisot (painter, 1841-1895), Fanny Claus (violinist, 1846-1877), et Antoine Guillemet (landscape painter, 1841-1918), 1868-1869.

Oil on canvas. H. 170 ; W. 124.5. Gustave Caillebotte Bequest, 1894.

The Impressionists
before 1870

In the early 1860s the private studio class run by Charles Gleyre, a painter of Swiss origin, became the focus of activity for a number of young painters. Auguste Renoir enrolled in 1861, to be joined shortly afterwards by Frédéric Bazille, newly arrived from Montpellier, and later Claude Monet and Alfred Sisley. These painters formed a group united by common ideals, in particular a hostility towards academic art and an inclination towards Realism. Renoir (1841-1919), with no family money behind him, managed to keep his head above water by painting portraits, among them one of his friend Sisley's father, accepted for the Salon of 1865. Renoir's lifelong attachment to the human figure is illustrated by *Le Garçon au chat (Boy with Cat)*, painted in the studio of his friend Frédéric Bazille. Although partly inspired by old masters and Courbet, this work bears comparison to Manet in terms of handling and palette. Bazille (1841-70), who died young in battle in the Franco-Prussian War, was another figure painter. *Réunion de*

59

59
Pierre-Auguste Renoir
Le Garçon au chat (Boy with Cat), 1868-1869.

Oil on canvas. H. 123 ; W. 66.
Purchased with the aid of
Philippe Meyer in 1992.

60

60
Frédéric Bazille
Réunion de famille (Family Gathering), 1867.

Oil on canvas. H. 152 ; W. 230. Purchased with support from Marc Bazille, the artist's brother, 1905.

61
Paul Cézanne
L'Avocat (L'oncle Dominique) (The Lawyer, Uncle Dominique), circa 1866.

Oil on canvas. H. 65 ; W. 54. Donated in lieu of estate duties, 1991.

61

62

62
Claude Monet
La Pie (The Magpie), circa
1868-1869.

Oil on canvas. H. 89 ; W. 130.
Purchased in 1984.

famille (Family Gathering), one of his most accomplished pictures, was executed in 1867 and exhibited at the Salon of 1868. It shows members of his family posing on the terrace of a house near Montpellier. A strong debt to Manet is apparent in the brilliance of the colouring, the bold presentation of human forms and the intensity of the light exaggerating the contrasts, but there is also an affinity with Monet, whom Bazille frequently accompanied on painting expeditions. Of all the group, Monet (1840-1926) was regarded as the most 'advanced'. As a young man in Le Havre he was decisively influenced by Boudin and Jongkind, who encouraged him to paint out of doors, and his early landscapes - which also owe much to Daubigny - have a freshness and confidence that did not escape the notice of the critics. Responding to Manet's picture of the same title, Monet painted his own large-scale composition *Le déjeuner sur l'herbe* (1865), two sections of which survive in the Musée d'Orsay, and then *Femmes au jardin (Women in the Garden),* rejected by the Salon of 1867, which includes a portrait of his future wife, Camille. This large and ambitious composition was started *in situ* as a *plein-air painting* (which, given the size of the canvas, was in itself a major achievement), the purpose being to retain the freshness of the original vision in the finished work; the canvas was in fact extensively reworked in the studio. The sharp silhouetting of the figures, the contrasts of light and

63

shade, and the choice of a subject from modern life with no anecdotal detail whatsoever, could not but offend the conservative Salon jury, who maintained an implacable hostility towards this style of painting which had grown up in the wake of Courbet and Manet. It fell to Zola to defend Monet's picture, just as he had pleaded the cause of Manet, Pissarro and Cézanne. Cézanne's *L'avocat (l'oncle Dominique) (Lawyer–Uncle Dominique)* is one of ten or so canvases in which the artist painted his uncle, often in fanciful pose or dress. This painting, executed swiftly with a palette knife, shows Cézanne embarking on what would become one of the major themes of his oeuvre–the representation of the human figure.

63
Claude Monet
*Déjeuner sur l'herbe
(Luncheon on the Grass)*,
1865-1866.

Oil on canvas. H. 248 ; W. 217.
Donated in lieu of estate duties,
1987.

64

64
Claude Monet
Femmes au jardin (Women in the Garden), 1866-1867.

Oil on canvas. H. 255 ; W. 205.
Purchased from the artist in 1921.

Drawing and
Watercolour

Complementing the collections of painting, sculpture and decorative arts in the Musée d'Orsay, there are also opportunities to see drawings by the various artists represented. These temporary exhibitions (it being possible to display the drawings only for restricted periods and in precise lighting conditions) are intended to serve very much as an introduction to the permanent collections of the Cabinet des Dessins in the Louvre. That vast repository includes examples of work, both individual items and major series, by most of the leading artists of the period covered by the Musée d'Orsay. A mention of just a few of the artists represented from the early years of that period will suggest something of the richness and diversity of the collections: the fantastical and meticulous storytelling of Gustave Doré is worlds away from the pungent Realism of Daumier, and the poetic Realism of Millet (particularly well represented here) contrasts with Impressionist sketches by Manet and Degas.

65
Gustave Doré
Catastrophe du mont Cervin, la chute (Tragedy on the Matterhorn: The Fall), 1865.

Pen and brown ink, wash in India and brown ink, highlights in white gouache.
H. 79.5 ; W. 59.5.
Gift of Mlle de Viefville, 1952.

65

66

67

66
Jean-François Millet
*Le Bouquet de marguerites
(The Bunch of Daisies)*,
1871-1874.

Pastel. H. 68 ; W. 83. Purchased
with dividends from the Bequest
of Mme Dol-Lair, 1949.

67
Honoré Daumier
*Le Défenseur (Counsel for
the Defence)*.

Pen and black ink, watercolour
and gouache over graphite.
H. 19 ; W. 29.5. Acquired in 1977.

68

69

70

68
Charles Baudelaire
Self-portrait, circa 1860.

Pen and India ink, red highlights.
H. 22.5 ; W. 15.
Purchased in 1988.

69
Edgar Degas
Edouard Manet.

Graphite and India ink wash.
H. 35 ; W. 20. Gift in 1988 of
M. Clément Rouart, who enjoyed
usufruct until 1992.

70
Edouard Manet
*Madame Manet sur un
canapé bleu (Mme Manet
on a Blue Sofa),* circa 1874.

Pastel. H. 49 ; W. 60.
Purchased in 1918.

71

71
Edouard Manet
*Femme dans un tub
(Woman in a Tub)*, 1878-
1879.

Pastel on cardboard.
H. 55 ; W. 45. Purchased in 1973.

Puvis de Chavannes, Moreau, Degas

72
Pierre Puvis de Chavannes
L'Eté (Summer), 1873.

Oil on canvas. H. 350 ; W. 507.
Purchased by the nation in 1873
for the Musée de Chartres,
attributed to the National
Museums in 1986.

Pierre Puvis de Chavannes and Gustave Moreau were both admirers, as young men, of the vast decorative works executed by Chassériau between 1844 and 1848 for the stairway of the Cour des Comptes. (These suffered war damage in 1871 and were removed in 1898, shortly before the building was demolished to make way for the Gare d'Orsay; today they are in the Louvre.)

Decoration is a strong element in the work of Puvis de Chavannes (1824-98), whether or not a painting was conceived with a particular location in mind. His *Eté (Summer)* could not be described as a naturalistic depiction of agricultural activity, nor is it precisely an allegory. In the words of the critic Georges Lafenestre, who saw the picture exhibited at the Salon of 1873, where it was acquired for the nation: 'This is not summer in Beauce or Brie. It is summer in an eternal land which the artist's soul inhabits; feelings there are no less intense, but they are more generalized.'

It is precisely this quality of timelessness. allied to a rejection of chiaroscuro in favour of pale, clear colours and flattened, simplified design, that made his work so attractive to the Symbolist painters of the latter years of the century, and in particular to Gauguin, Maillol and the Nabis. *Le pauvre pêcheur (The Poor Fisherman)*, of 1881, was initially greeted with mild puzzlement, before being hailed as the 'ultimate emblem of poverty' *(synthèse de la misère)* when it entered the Musée du Luxembourg in 1887.

Like Puvis de Chavannes, Edgar Degas (1834-1917) abandoned his law studies in order to concentrate on painting and, also like him, travelled in Italy, where some of his relations lived. It was during a visit to Florence, in 1858, to see his aunt Laure Bellelli (née De Gas - it was the painter himself who adopted the form Degas) that he started *La famille Bellelli (The Bellelli Family)*. This ambitious composition draws on the tradition of the posed family photograph. Even more strikingly, it echoes the style of Ingres, for whom Degas had a profound admiration. The final canvas was preceded by numerous sketches. drawn and painted, both of details and of the whole picture. The work was discovered in the artists studio after his death and was acquired for the national museums when the contents were put up for auction. The painting demonstrates

Pierre Puvis de Chavannes
*Le Pauvre Pêcheur (The
Poor Fisherman)*, 1881.
Oil on canvas. H. 155.5 ; W. 192.5.
Purchased in 1887.

74

74
Edgar Degas
*Sémiramis construisant
Babylone (Semiramis
Building Babylon),* 1861.
Oil on canvas. H. 151 ; W. 258.
Purchased in 1918.

Degas' consummate skill in portraiture, as alert to details of
contemporary life as to the psychology of his sitters. A number
of other portraits of his family and friends are also to be seen in
the Musée d'Orsay.

In the early years of his career Degas aspired to the status of
a history painter, as witness his *Sémiramis construisant Babylone (Semiramis Building Babylon)* of 1861; although this particular canvas was not exhibited at the Salon, it is typical of the
series of history compositions exhibited by the young painter in
the 1860s. At that time Degas had much in common with Gustave Moreau (1826-98), with whom he became friendly in 1859.
Moreau was a pupil of Picot and knew Chassériau well. From
1864 onwards he was hugely successful at the Salon: the Musée
d'Orsay has in its possession his *Jason,* from the Salon of 1865,
and the *Orphée (Orpheus)* shown there in 1866. The latter was
selected for permanent exhibition in the Musée du Luxembourg, and was regarded at the time as a masterpiece worthy of
the Renaissance. The iconographic invention of the young
Thracian girl reverently bearing the head and lyre of the bard
slain by the Maenads marks one of the first appearances of a
theme used widely by the Symbolists in the second half of the
nineteenth century, to represent the artist (Orpheus or John
the Baptist) whose ideas and creations live on beyond his death.

75

Gustave Moreau
L'Apparition (The Apparition), 1876.
Watercolour. H. 106 ; W. 72.
Gift of Charles Hayem, 1898.

76

Gustave Moreau
Orphée (Orpheus), 1865.
Oil on wood. H. 154 ; W. 99.5.
Purchased in 1866.

76

77

77
Edgar Degas
La Famille Bellelli (The Bellilli Family) Baron Gennaro Bellelli, his wife (née Laure De Gas, the artist's aunt) and their daughters. Begun in Florence in 1858, perhaps exhibited at the Salon of 1867.

Oil on canvas. H. 200 ; W. 250. Purchased in 1918 with support from Comte and Comtesse de Fels, and thanks to René De Gas.

Whistler

James Abbott McNeill Whistler (1834-1903) was just over twenty when he left the United States and went to study painting in France. Thenceforth he was to divide his life between Paris and London. A friend of Courbet and of Fantin-Latour - who painted him alongside Baudelaire, Manet and others in his *Homage to Delacroix* - Whistler was from the outset inclined towards Realism, and his work therefore received a frosty reception in official circles. He was, too, a fervent admirer of Far Eastern art, and in particular Japanese prints, whose introduction to the West had such a profound influence on so many European artists. This love of decorative simplicity was reflected in the extreme delicacy of his palette, founded in exquisite harmonies of finely graduated, understated colour. Famous for his views of the Thames, painted in a quivering haze reminiscent of some of the effects achieved by Monet at a certain period, Whistler was also a successful portraitist. His *Arrangement en gris et noir, portrait de la mère de l'artiste (Arrangement in Grey and Black, Portrait of the Artist's Mother)*, of 1871, entered the French national collections in 1891 thanks to the efforts of his friend the poet Stéphane Mallarmé and of the critic Théodore Duret, who knew Manet and the Impressionists and admired Whistler's work. This rather austere painting has become the artist's best-known work.

78
James Abbott McNeill Whistler
Arrangement en gris et noir n° 1 ou *La mère de l'artiste (Arrangement in Grey and Black: Portrait of the Artist's Mother)*, 1871.
Oil on canvas. H. 144.3 ; W. 162.5.
Purchased in 1891.

78

Photography

Long overlooked and even now largely neglected, the photography of the nineteenth century is given proper coverage for the first time with the opening of the Musée d'Orsay. The displays have been organized to illustrate the significant developments in the history of photography, both in France and abroad, starting with the daguerreotype and ending with the snapshot and the rise of the 'pictorialist' movement. At this point the Musée National d'Art Moderne in the Centre Pompidou takes over, with the abstract and experimental photography that first appeared in Europe and America towards the end of the First World War.

When work was started on assembling the Musée d'Orsay collection, in 1979, it was decided to concentrate specifically on photography as a creative art, thus supplying a different emphasis from the archive of the Bibliothèque Nationale, which, according to a law passed in 1851, receives copies of all commercially used photographs. The principal criterion of 'artistic' quality is originality in the interpretation of subject matter. and yet some of the most imaginative uses of the medium in the nineteenth century were in the form of documentary records - one thinks in particular of the views of Egypt by J. B. Greene (1832-57) or the Parisian scenes of Eugène Atget (1857-1923). The museum is not interested exclusively in the work of professional photographers; it is also concerned with artists working in other fields who at certain times experimented with photography for particular purposes of their own, whether visual artists (Degas, Bonnard, Gallé) or writers (such as Victor Hugo or Lewis Carroll).

The Musée d'Orsay collections are particularly well endowed with the works of the so-called 'primitives', active first in England and later in France when photographs first began to be printed on paper (c. 1850-60). Within that short period the expressive potential of the new medium was explored with startling inventiveness, scope and mastery.

79

79
Nadar (Félix Tournachon)
*Portrait d'une Antillaise
(Portrait of a West Indian
Woman)*, circa 1855.

Salt print from wet-collodion glass-plate negative. H. 25 ; W. 19. Purchased in 1981.

80
Gustave Le Gray
Le Vapeur (The Steamer),
1857.

Albumen print from wet-collodion glass plate negative. H. 33 ; W. 41.3. Purchased in 1985.

Charles Hugo
Victor Hugo sur un rocher,
Jersey (Victor Hugo on a
Rock, Jersey), 1853.

Albumen salt print from glass
negative. H. 15.4 ; W. 21.6.
Gift of Marie-Thérèse and André
Jammes, 1984.

81

82

Thomas Annan
Plate from the album
"Photographs of the Old
Closes and Streets of
Glasgow": Close n° 83
High Street, 1868-1871.

Albumen print from wet-
collodion glass-plate negative.
H. 28.2 ; W. 23. Purchased in
1983.

83

Jean Charles Langlois,
Frédéric Martens,
Léon-Eugène Mehedin
Three Plates from a
panorama of Sebastopol
taken from the Malakoff
Tower (Crimean War,
November 1855).

Albumen salt print from a waxed
paper negative. H. 35 ; W. 31
(average per image). Purchased
in 1982 thanks to a grant from
the Mission pour le Patrimoine
Photographique (Direction du
Patrimoine).
The Panorama was composed
of fourteen calotypes placed end
to end to form a 360° view.

82

83

84

84
Edouard Baldus
*Groupe dans un parc
(Group in a Park)*, 1857.

Albumen print from wet-collodion glass-plate negative. H. 29 ; W. 40.9. Gift of the Kodak-Pathé Foundation, 1983.

85
Lewis Carroll (Charles Lutwidge Dodgson)
Xie Kitchin Asleep,
12 June 1873.

Albumen print from wet-collodion glass-plate negative. H. 12 ; W. 14.5. Purchased in 1982.

85

86
Edouard-Denis Baldus
*La destruction de la
Grande Galerie
(Demolishing the Grande
Galerie)*, 1861-1865.

Albumen print from wet-collodion glass-plate negative. H. 45 ; W. 39. Purchased in 1988.

86

81

87

88

87

Nadar (Félix Tournachon)
*Portrait of Théophile
Gautier in White Jacket,*
circa 1855.

Salt print from wet-collodion
glass-plate negative.
H. 28.6 ; W. 21.2.
Purchased in 1991.

88

Nadar (Félix Tournachon)
*Portrait of Auguste
Préault,* circa 1855.

Salt print on glass-plate negative.
H. 23.4 ; W. 17.2. Purchased in
1991.

89

Nadar (Félix Tournachon)
*Portrait of Charles
Baudelaire in a Louis XIII
Armchair,* circa 1855.

Salt print from glass-plate
negative. H. 21.2 ; W. 16.1.
Purchased in 1991.

89

82

90

90
William Henry Fox Talbot
*Trees Reflected in Water,
Lacock Abbey,* circa 1843.

Calotype, salt print from paper
negative. H. 16.4 ; W. 19.1.
Donated by the Commission
Nationale de la Photographie,
1994.

Painting:
eclecticism

The huge canvas by Thomas Couture (1815-79), *Romains de la décadence (Romans of the Decadence)*, commissioned in 1846 and exhibited at the Salon of 1847, is based on a quotation from one of Juvenal's satires: 'More cruel than war, vice battened on Rome and avenged the conquered world.' The composition draws on established formal models, and there are clear references to Tiepolo, Rubens, Poussin and, in particular, Veronese. However, it is interesting that Couture had no hesitation in showing his figures in unheroic poses.

This was in contrast to the idealism of those artists who exactly conformed to what they were taught at the Ecole des Beaux-Arts, where the ultimate reward, for winners of the Prix de Rome a period of residence in Italy at the Villa Medicis. Among such prize-winners were Alexandre Cabanel (1823-89), honoured in 1845; William Bouguereau (1825-1905) and Paul Baudry (1826-86), in 1850; Elie Debunay (1821-91), in 1856; and Henri Regnault(1843-71), in 1866. Success at this early stage was the guarantee of a brilliant career. Thus in 1863, already the recipient of a Salon medal, Cabanel was elected to the Institut de France and made a professor at the Ecole des

91
Thomas Couture
*Romains de la décadence
(Romans of the
Decadence)*, 1847.
Oil on canvas. H. 472 ; W. 772.
Purchased in 1847.

92

92
Alexandre Cabanel
Naissance de Vénus (Birth of Venus), 1863.

Oil on canvas. H. 130 ; W. 225. Purchased by Napoléon III in 1863 and attributed to the National Museums in 1879.

Beaux-Arts. In the same year he had enormous success at the Salon with his *Naissance de Venus (Birth of Venus)*, which was immediately bought by Napoleon III for his private collection.

Cabanel's pupil, Regnault, was unusual in that he spent only two years in Italy before moving on to Spain. All official residents of the Villa Medicis were obliged to make regular submissions of their work. Regnault sent his fourth-year work from Tangiers: *Exécution sans jugement sous les rois maures de Grenade (Summary Execution under the Moorish Kings of Granada)*. Such was the youthful painter's fame that his death in battle at Buzenval in 1871 shocked the artistic world.

One of the finest examples of Second Empire history painting is Delaunay's *La Peste à Rome (Plague in Rome)*, exhibited at the Salon of 1869. The canvas was the culmination of many years of work. Life drawings were made for every single figure, and there are numerous smaller versions and preparatory studies which reveal how the composition developed in dramatic intensity, ultimately focusing on the central group of exterminating angels.

94

93
Henri Regnault
*Exécution sans jugement
sous les rois maures de
Grenade (Summary
Execution under the
Moorish Kings of
Granada)*, 1870.

Oil on canvas. H. 302 ; W. 146.
Purchased in 1872.

94
Jules-Elie Delaunay
*Peste à Rome (Plague in
Rome)*, based on the story of
Saint Sebastian in Jacobus da
Voragine's *Golden Legend*, 1869.

Oil on canvas. H. 131 ; W. 176.5.
Purchased in 1869.

96

95
William Bouguereau
La Danse (The Dance),
salon decoration, 1856.

Oil and wax on canvas.
H. 367 ; W. 185. Gift of Captain
Peter Moore, 1981.

96
Auguste Clésinger
*Femme piquée par un
serpent (Woman Bitten by
a Snake),* 1847.

Marble. H. 56.5 ; W. 180 ; D. 70.
Purchased in 1931.

Sculpture: eclecticism

Sculptural eclecticism was heralded during the reign of Louis-Philippe by the scandalously lewd pose of *La Femme piquée par un serpent (Woman Bitten by a Snake)* by Clésinger (1814–1883), exhibited at the Salon of 1847.

French society was transformed by the industrial revolution that took place during the Second Empire. Fortunes changed hands, and the newly affluent bourgeoisie set about creating its own style. Needing confirmation of their status, its members tended to look to the past to provide models. Historical subjects were the fashion in the nineteenth century: writers, and later artists, scoured earlier civilizations for themes they could adapt to their own purposes. Such evidence of culture and good taste was warmly received by their new patrons.

The Hellenistic bronzes of Pompeii, and Giovanni da Bologna's, *Mercury*, were the inspiration to Alexandre Falguière (1831-1900) and Hippolyte Moulin (1832-84) for their figures of athletic young men, exhibited at the Salon of 1864. Together with Paul Dubois and Antonin Mercié, these two sculptors formed a group known as *Les Florentins*, in acknowledgment of their debt to Tuscany. Many of the drawings of Dubois (1829-

97

98

97
Ernest Christophe
La Comédie humaine ou *Le Masque (The Human Comedy,* or, *The Mask)*, 1857-1876.

Marble. H. 245 ; W. 85 ; D. 72. Purchased in 1876.

98
Alexandre Falguière
Vainqueur au combat de coqs (Winner of the Cock Fight), 1864.

Bronze. H. 174 ; W. 100 ; p. 82. Purchased in 1864.

99
Albert-Ernest Carrier-Belleuse
Hébé (Hebe), 1869.

Marble. H. 207 ; W. 146 ; D. 85. Acquired in 1869.

100
Charles Cordier
Nègre du Soudan (Negro from Sudan), 1857.

Bronze and onyx.
H. 96 ; l. 66 ; D. 36.
Purchased in 1857.

101
Paul Dubois
Chanteur florentin (Florentine Singer), 1865.

Silver-plated bronze.
H. 155 ; W. 58 ; D. 50.
Commissioned in 1865 and
exhibited at the 1867 World Fair
in Paris.

1905) were based on works by Benozzo Gozzoli. Dubois' *Petit chanteur du xve siècle (Florentine Singer)* won the gold medal at the Salon of 1865, arousing such enthusiasm that a quarrel broke out between the Emperor's cousin Princess Mathilde and the Director of the Beaux-Arts, Count Nieuwerkerke, as to who should have the first cast; it was the Princess who emerged victorious. Small replicas of the figure were produced both in bronze (Barbedienne) and in unglazed porcelain (Sèvres). Mercié (1845-1916), while still technically a student in residence at the Villa Medicis in Rome, was awarded the Légion d'Honneur for his second-year work, a *David* sheathing his sword, a superbly flowing and developed human figure.

Albert-Ernest Carrier-Belleuse (1824-87) also used a classical model for his finest relief, *Hebe et l'aigle (Hebe and the Eagle)*. *The Comédie humaine (The Human Comedy)* by Ernest Christophe (1827-92) inspired Baudelaire's thoughts on the 'correspondences' between poetry and sculpture, in Chant XXI of *Les Fleurs du mal* of 1857.

Love of history in this period was matched by a taste for far-off places. Charles Cordier (1827-1905) obtained funding for a series of expeditions, the most tangible result of which was the lavish use, in his sculpture, of onyx mined in the newly opened Algerian quarries. The employment of rich, coloured stone in statuary was then much in vogue, reflecting the affluence of the age.

Carpeaux

102

'A statue conceived by the poet of the *Divine Comedy* and created by the begetter of Moses: that would indeed be a masterpiece of the human spirit', wrote Jean-Baptiste Carpeaux (1827-75) in 1854, the year in which he won the Prix de Rome at his tenth attempt. Carpeaux is of course referring to Dante and Michelangelo, who were revered by the sculptors of the latter half of the nineteenth century and were the direct inspiration for his own *Ugolin (Ugolino)*. This piece was originally conceived as Carpeaux's official submission in his final year of residence at the Villa Medicis, and, although it did not conform to the rules laid down by the Académie de France in Rome, was recognized as a masterpiece by Count Nieuwerkerke, himself a sculptor. Through him, Carpeaux was introduced to the Imperial court, and though not the official portraitist (a post held by Jean-Auguste Barre) he produced a number of vivid terracottas of Napoleon III and the Empress. His sole official commission was for a full-length marble statue of the Prince Imperial with his dog. The three figures shown here give an indication of Carpeaux's talents - qualities of observation and lively expression – which are equally apparent in his paintings. Naturally enough, major public commissions went to winners of the Prix de Rome, and there was no lack of new facades to decorate in the Second Empire. Carpeaux sculpted the allegorical figure of *La France impériale protégeant l'Agriculture et les Sciences (Imperial France protecting Agriculture and the Sciences)* to crown the south front of the new Pavillon de Flore of the Louvre, designed by Hector Lefuel. Here too his admiration for Michelangelo was evident:

102
Jean-Baptiste Carpeaux
Le Prince impérial et son chien Néro (The Prince Imperial and his Dog Nero), 1865.

Marble. H. 140.2 ; W. 65.4 ; D. 61.5. Gift of Mme Deutsch de la Meurthe, 1930.

103
Jean-Baptiste Carpeaux
L'Impératrice Eugénie et le prince impérial (Empress Eugénie and the Prince Imperial).

Terracotta. H. 26.1 ; W. 14.5 ; D. 13.8. Gift of Jacques Doucet, 1908.

103 bis
Jean-Baptiste Carpeaux
Napoléon III, circa 1864.

Terracotta. H. 17.5 ; W. 7.8 ; D. 7.5. Gift of Jacques Doucet, 1908.

103

103 bis

105

104
104
Jean-Baptiste Carpeaux
Ugolin (Ugolino).

Bronze. H. 194 ; W. 148 ; D. 119.
Commissioned in 1862, Salon of
1863.

105
Jean-Baptiste Carpeaux
*La France impériale proté-
geant l'Agriculture et les
Sciences (Imperial France
Protecting Agriculture and
Science).*

Plaster. H. 268 ; W. 427 ; D. 162.
Commissioned in 1863, Salon of
1866, purchased in 1892.

the oculi were encircled by children bearing palms, and,
beneath them, the relief of Flora was a splendid tribute to
Rubens, a celebration of fleshly form and life. The theme of
Flora surrounded by a ring of children was taken up as the
central motif of *La danse (The Dance)*. Commissioned for the
new Opéra by his old student friend Charles Garnier in 1863
(although the official commission for a 'group of three figures'
was not issued until 1865), the relief is full of movement and
dynamism, reflecting the detailed work Carpeaux put into his
many preparatory sketches and maquettes. The group's animation and verve could not have provided a greater contrast
with the contributions from François Jouffroy, Claude
Guillaume and Jean Perraud, the Academicians commissioned
to decorate the other three piers. When the work was unveiled
in 1869 there was a popular outcry. The prudes joined forces
with the opponents of the regime and demanded action. Garnier himself, apparently, was 'lost in admiration for the vivid
composition, the life-like modelling, and said, "Well, if the building suffers a little from my sculptor's exuberance, that will be
a small price to pay, but the price would be huge if I stuck
rigidly to my ideas and deprived France of a work that will certainly be a masterpiece." In the end, Garnier was obliged to
bow to pressure from above, and another group was commissioned from the sculptor Charles Gumery. But the war of 1870
and the death of Carpeaux, at the age of forty-seven, meant that
the substitution was never effected. Gumery's group was placed
in the Musée d'Angers. In 1964, threatened by pollution, Carpeaux's original was removed to the Louvre and replaced by a
copy.

The new Opera House

107

On 29 December 1860 Napoleon III decreed the construction of a new Paris opera house as a matter of 'public interest'. The decision was overdue: the cramped building in the rue Le Peletier had never been regarded as anything more than a temporary base, and a number of abortive schemes had been drawn up over the past century for moves to a variety of locations. The winning design in the competition launched in December 1860 was submitted by an unknown young architect, Charles Garnier. The siting of the Opera House in a newly developed neighbourhood meant that Garnier had to deal with Haussmann's massed, uniform facades. The great achievement of Garnier's design is that, although standing in the heart of an area that is a monument to the efficiency of Second Empire town-planning, the Opera triumphantly sets itself apart from every other building in Paris, rejecting straight lines in favour of flowing curves, austerity in favour of ornamental exuberance, regularity in favour of the picturesque, grey in favour of sumptuous polychromatic effects. In the interior, Garnier transforms the spectator's experience, as he walks from the entrance to his seat, into a piece of French grand opera, conceived in architectural terms: extravagant dramatic effects, contrasts of light and shade, alternation of intimate passages with grandiose tableaux.

106
Jean-Baptiste Carpeaux
La Danse (The Dance),
1869.

Stone. H. 420 ; W. 298 ; D. 145. Commissioned in 1865, unveiled in 1869, transported from the Opera to the Louvre in 1964 and from the Louvre to the Musée d'Orsay in 1986.

107
Jean-Baptiste Carpeaux
Charles Garnier (1825-1898), architect of the new Paris Opera House, 1869.

Bronze. H. 67.6 ; W. 54.5 ; D. 33.6. Bequest of Mme Charles Garnier, 1921.

108
Cross-section of the Opera,
produced by the Richard Peduzzi atelier, 1986. Plaster.

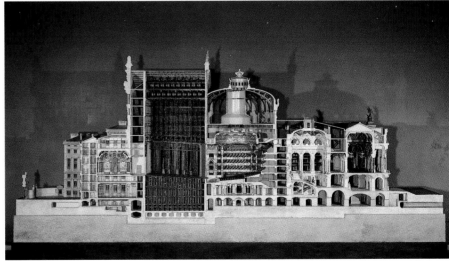

108

109
Alphonse Nicolas Crépinet
*Proposal for the new Paris
Opera House,* 1861.

Graphite and watercolour.
Unsuccessful submission, placed
second after that by Charles
Garnier.
H. 50.6 ; W. 68.9.
Purchased in 1983.

Architecture and
Town-planning

110 and 111
Victor Ruprich-Robert
Floral ornamentation: Ash Bud; Thistle, circa 1866-1869.

Crayon and graphite.
H. 41.5 ; W. 33.8. Gift of the Ruprich-Robert family, 1981.

112
Max Berthelin
Palais de l'Industrie, cross section, 1854.

Pen and black ink, watercolour.
H. 31.1 ; W. 67.3. Purchased in 1979.

In architecture, the second half of the nineteenth century was a time of expansion. There was extensive urban redevelopment, not only in Haussmann's Paris but in comparable programmes in provincial France and abroad. A vast construction programme was undertaken - railway stations, factories, town halls, museums, schools and colleges, grand hotels. Technology was making rapid strides; iron was in widespread use, and concrete began to make an appearance. The architecture of this period can all too easily seem to be bogged down in a more or less slavish imitation of bygone styles. Yet the historicism of Eugene Viollet-le-Duc (1814-79) or Victor Ruprich-Robert (1859–1953) cannot simply be dis-

110   111

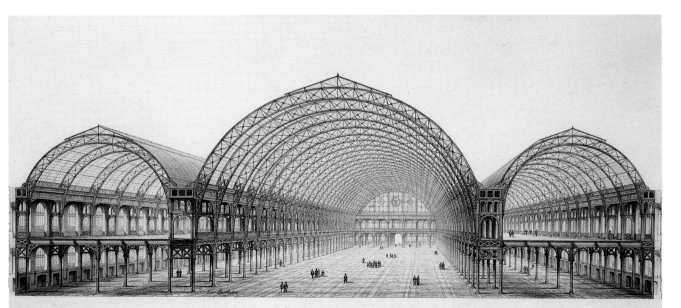

112

113
Armand Bourgade *Picture-poem in the form of the Eiffel Tower*, 1889.

H. 80 ; W. 57.
Eiffel archives. Gift of
Mlle Solange Granet,
Mme Bernard Granet and her
children, descendants of Gustave
Eiffel, 1981.

113

114

115

114
Adolphe Alphand, Jean
Darcel, Emile Reiber
*Design for a wrought iron
tower for the artesian well
in Passy*, 1857.

Watercolour with white
highlights in gouache.
H. 98 ; W. 67.
Purchased in 1988.

115
Monduit Company
Designs for finials, late 19th
century.

Pen and black ink, grey wash,
white highlights.
H. 49.8 ; W. 79.7. Gift of
Mme G. Pasquier-Monduit, 1983.

116

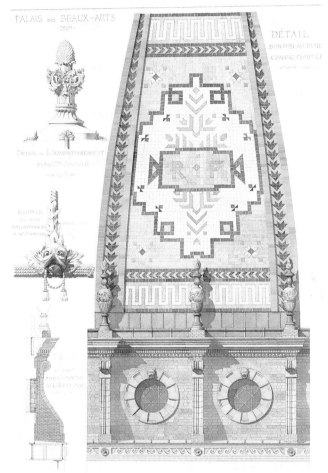

117

116

Jean-Camille Formigé
*Palais des Beaux-Arts,
World Fair of 1889. Corner
pavilion facing the Seine.*

Pen and black ink, black and
pink wash.
H. 99 ; W. 66.4.
Gift of the Société des Amis
d'Orsay, 1991.

117

Jean-Camille Formigé
*Palais des Beaux-Arts,
World Fair of 1889.
Exterior decoration of the
large domes (detail of one
section of a dome).*

Pen and black ink, grey wash and
watercolour.
H. 96.5 ; W. 65.5.
Gift of the Société des Amis
d'Orsay, 1991.

missed as a sterile reproduction of the forms of a previous age;
these architects were, in their own way, as interested as was the
Arts and Crafts Movement in England in extending their designs to include even the smallest detail of interior decoration.
Using medieval architecture as a source of new design ideas,
they paved the way for the movement we now call Art Nouveau. Among the more prominent landmarks of the architecture of this period are buildings erected for the World Fairs
held in Paris between 1855 and 1900, notably the Palais de
l'Industrie (1855) and the Eiffel Tower (1889).

118

118
Jean-Camille Formigé
*Palais des Beaux-Arts,
World Fair of 1889. A bay
of the central porch
overlooking the garden.*

Graphite, pen and black ink,
watercolour. H. 102 ; W. 65.8.
Gift of the Société des Amis
d'Orsay, 1991.

Decorative arts: eclecticism

119

Eclecticism embodies the belief that all styles are equal. This was an emergent trend in the mid nineteenth century, and corresponded to the aspirations of a rising bourgeoisie, who looked to the past or to the colonial experience for their models. As industry and commerce boomed, so the stylistic blend gained an international currency. The World Fairs, with their exhibitions of artefacts from many different countries, prompted a realization of the dire consequences of over-rapid industrialization, and a number of ventures were started which aimed to reconcile Utility with Beauty. Design schools, societies for the promotion of design, and museums of applied arts were established; competitions and special exhibitions were held, and reviews and pattern-books were published. Eclecticism was a source of creative regeneration, since it encouraged designers to measure themselves against the geniuses of antiquity, to take as their standard the very best that history and the contemporary world could offer: it also fostered a revival of interest in nature. Hence commercial designers show a variety of stylistic emphases within a framework of Naturalism: Sévin (Neoclassical); Avisseau and Frullini (Neo-Renaissance); Schilt and Cremer (Neo-Rococo); Deck (Islamic); Braquemond and Rousseau (Japanese), to name but a few.

The big industrial firms hired the best designers - architects, sculptors, painters and above all ornamentalists - whose industrial work was exhibited and won awards. What these artists had in common, in spite of their apparent diversity of style, was a desire to think on a large scale, a concern for quality, a superb audacity in the way they juxtaposed motifs or used unusual combinations of materials and colours, and an enthusiasm for new technical developments. As well as one-off pieces commissioned by individual patrons or destined for international exhibitions, there began to appear works designed with mass-production in mind, quickly produced and available to a wider public. At the other end of the spectrum, the traditions of craftsmanship were maintained by a small number of producers who rejected mechanization and the division of labour.

120

121

122

120

François-Désiré Froment-Meurice, goldsmith, **Jacques-Félix Duban**, architect, **Adolphe-Victor Geoffroy-Dechaume**, sculptor, **Jean-Jacques Feuchère**, sculptor, **Michel Liénard**, decorator
Jewel casket (one of a pair), 1849.

Partly gilded silver, painted enamel, emeralds and garnets.
H. 42.6 ; W. 35.8 ; D. 27.5.
Purchased in 1981.
From a dressing-table set commissioned for the wedding of the Duchess of Parma, granddaughter of Charles X, in November 1845, completed only in 1851.

122

Christofle & Co., goldsmiths, **Mathurin Moreau**, sculptor, **Auguste Madroux**, decorator
Ornamental vase depicting "The Education of Achilles", circa 1867.

Partly gilded silver.
H. 75 ; W. 26 ; D. 13. Presented by Napoléon III to the Cercle des Patineurs to serve as trophy for the annual pigeon shoot organized by the Cercle, in 1867.
Purchased in 1982.

121

C.J. Avisseau, ceramicist; **O. Guillaume de Rochebrune**, designer
Large cup and platter. Faïence with coloured relief and inlaid decoration.

Cup H. 34.5 ; diam. 26.5 ;
Platter H. 8 ; diam. 51.5.
Purchased in 1983.
Based on a design by Rochebrune, this large cup featured in the 1855 World Fair.

123

Charles Guillaume Diehl, cabinetmaker, **Jean Brandely**, industrial designer, **Emmanuel Fremiet**, sculptor
Medal cabinet, circa 1867.

Cedar, walnut, ebony, ivory, bronze and galvanized silver-plated copper. H. 238 ; W. 151 ; D. 60. Purchased in 1873.
Fremiet's original plaster cast of the central relief depicting "The Triumphal Entry of Merewig into Châlons-sur-Marne" was donated by Madame René Martin in 1973.

124

124
Philippe-Joseph Brocard
Basin, 1871.

Blown glass, glazed and gilded
decoration, original stand of
ebonized wood. H. 20 ; W. 39.
Purchased in 1987.

125

125
**Manufacture de Creil et
Montereau, Félix
Bracquemond**, painter and
engraver, **Eugène Rousseau**,
editor
Centrepiece, 1867.

Faience with printed and painted
underglaze decoration.
H. 15 ; W. 62.2 ; D. 42.2.
Purchased in 1984.
Part of the 'Japanese' dinner
service commissioned from
Bracquemond by Rousseau in
1866, manufactured by Leveille
up to 1903.

126
François-Eugène Rousseau,
editor, **Appert brothers**,
master glassmakers
Vase ("Teardrop model"),
designed circa 1875-1878.

Tinted glass, appliqués, with
engraved, painted, glazed and
gilded decoration. H. 25 ; W. 23 ;
D. 5. Purchased in 1985.

126

127

128

127
Christofle & Co., firm
headed by Henri Bouilhet
and Paul Christofle, Emile-
Auguste Reiber, industrial
designer
*Candelabrum (one of a
pair),* circa 1873.

Bronze with patina, gilding and
cloisonné enamel.
H. 56 ; W. 31.5 ; D. 31.5.
Purchased in 1982.
Part of a set originally including
a flower-stand, executed for the
Vienna World Fair, 1873.

128
Edouard Lièvre, designer,
Edouard Detaille, painter
*Cupboard on supporting
table,* circa 1877.

Rosewood, chased and gilded
bronze, engraved iron, oil on
wood, glass. H. 210 ; W. 110 ;
D. 57. Purchased in 1981.

Arts and Crafts

A W. N. Pugin (1812-52), whose principles of honest, functional architecture were derived from a study of Gothic art, sowed the seeds for the Arts and Crafts Movement that grew up in England from the 1860s onwards as a reaction against the dehumanizing effects of mechanization.

Thomas Carlyle and John Ruskin maintained an idealistically rigid view of society in their condemnation of machinery, whereas others, such as Robert Owen (the father of English Socialism) and Henry Cole (organizer of the first World Fair, the Great Exhibition of 1851, and one of the pioneers of industrial design) adopted a more pragmatic approach.

It is to William Morris (1834-96) that the credit goes for translating theory into practice. In 1861 he set up his own firm and devised a system of production that integrated craftwork with mechanization, making it possible to produce both everyday household articles and luxury goods. Morris attracted many imitators and disciples: some, such as Arthur Heygate Mackmurdo (founder of the Century Guild, 1882), Walter Crane (Art Workers' Guild, 1884), Charles Robert Ashbee (Guild of Handicraft, 1888) and Ernest Gimson (Kenton and Co., 1890),

129
J.W. Hukin & J. T. Heath, London and Birmingham; C. Dresser, designer
Soup tureen, patented in 1880.
Silver-plated metal, ebony. H. 21 ; W. 31 ; D. 23.5. Purchased in 1985.

130
Morris & Co., London; William Morris, decorator
Painted wood panelling (detail), circa 1880.
From the home of the Earl of Carlisle. Palace Green, London. Purchased in 1979.
The decor of the earl's dining-room also included a series of paintings by Burne-Jones, *Cupid and Psyche* (City Art Gallery, Birmingham).

131
Morris, Marshall, Faulkner & Co, London; P. Webb, architect and designer
Table
Polished oak, brass. H. 73 ; W. 167 ; D. 61. Purchased in 1979.
Philip Webb was a partner in Morris's firm from 1861, designing most of the furniture in the early years of the firm.

129

130

ultimately foundered on the contradictions inherent in the Arts and Crafts Movement, which tended to create luxury craft items beyond the pockets of all but the prosperous few.

Others, among them Edward William Godwin (1833-86) and Christopher Dresser (1834-1904), chose to work in association with industrial concerns; strongly influenced by Japanese design, they developed a stripped-down Anglo-Japanese style that was ideally suited to mass-production.

Almost all these designers were trained, if not practicing, architects, which gave them an all-encompassing vision of a fine lifestyle available, theoretically at least, to all.

131

132

132
Claude Monet
*Les Déchargeurs de char-
bon (Stevedores)*, 1875.

Oil on canvas. H. 55 ; W. 66.
Donated in lieu of estate duties,
1993.

Impressionism

133
Claude Monet
*Régates à Argenteuil
(Sailboats at Argenteuil),*
circa 1872.

Oil on canvas. H. 48 ; W. 75.
Gustave Caillebotte Bequest,
1894.

Tired of constant rebuffs from the Salon jury, a few artists decided in the spring of 1874 to stage an independent exhibition of their works in rooms on the Boulevard des Capucines in Paris. Among them were Edgar Degas, Auguste Renoir, Camille Pissarro, Paul Cézanne, Alfred Sisley, Armand Guillaumin, Berthe Morisot, and Claude Monet, who showed a canvas called *Impression soleil levant (Impression: Sunrise)*. An incensed critic coined the mocking epithet 'impressionist', and the name stuck. There was one notable absentee from their ranks, a painter who had crossed swords more than once with the Salon jury and chose not to risk further offence. This was Edouard Manet, who, by public and critics alike, was regarded as the leader of the group, which assembled regularly at the Café Guerbois and later the Café de la Nouvelle Athènes. The experiment of a group exhibition was repeated in 1876, 1877, 1879, 1880, 1881, 1882 and 1886. Although there was some internal dissension and a number of defections, there were always newcomers keen to participate, among them Gustave Caillebotte (1848-94), in 1876, who helped his friends by

133

134

buying their paintings. He left his magnificent collection to the
nation in 1894, and so ensured, in the face of fierce opposition
at the time, the, presence in the state collections of a superb
body of Impressionist painting, today one of the glories of the
Musée d'Orsay. In 1879, at the time of the fourth independent
exhibition, the group was joined by Mary Cassatt, a friend of
Degas, and also by Albert Lebourg and Paul Gauguin, closely
associated with Pissarro. The participation of Georges Seurat
and Paul Signac in the last exhibition, of 1886, effectively marked the end of one era and the beginning of the next.

It was only because of the loyalty of a small number of collectors and critics, among them Paul Durand-Ruel, that these
painters managed to survive the hardships of those difficult
years. Most of them had started their careers in the 1860s and
had reached artistic maturity without receiving official recognition. By then, though they were still united in their opposition to academic art and in their desire to be painters of the
modern age, their divergent personalities had begun to lead
them in very different directions.

Monet moved away from huge canvases and figure painting in order to devote himself to studying the vibrant effects
of light, concentrating on landscapes of the Seine valley
around Argenteuil - a magnet for all the Impressionists, and
even for Manet, in the early 1870s. Monet's *Régates à Argenteuil (Sailing Boats at Argenteuil)*, which has all the spontaneity and charm of a sketch, and his *Coquelicots (Wild
Poppies)*, a subtly rhythmic composition echoing the forms of
two figures in a landscape - these are paintings that typify
Impressionism at its peak.

Monet also painted scenes of Paris, and the wonderfully
luminous series based on the Gare Saint-Lazare - a modern

135

135
Pierre-Auguste Renoir
*Bal du Moulin de la
Galette (Dancing at
Moulin de la Galette)*, 1876.
Oil on canvas. H. 131 ; W. 175.
Gustave Caillebotte Bequest,
1894.

136

136
Claude Monet
*La Gare Saint-Lazare
(Saint Lazare Station),*
1877.

Oil on canvas. H. 75.5 ; W. 104.
Gustave Caillebotte Bequest,
1894.

137
Claude Monet
*La Rue Montorgueil, à
Paris (Rue Montorgueil
in Paris).* Celebrations on
June 30, 1878.

Oil on canvas. H. 81 ; W. 50.5.
Donated in lieu of estate duties,
1982.

137

138

139

140

138
Camille Pissarro
Les Toits rouges, coin de village, effet d'hiver (Red Roofs, Edge of Village, Winter), 1877.

Oil on canvas. H. 54.5 ; W. 65. Gustave Caillebotte Bequest, 1894.

140
Berthe Morisot
Le Berceau (The Cradle), 1872.

Oil on canvas. H. 56 ; W. 46. Purchased in 1930.

139
Paul Cézanne
La Maison du pendu (House of the Hanged Man), Auvers-sur-Oise, 1873.

Oil on canvas. H. 55 ; W. 66. Isaac de Camondo Bequest, 1911.

141
Claude Monet
Les Coquelicots (Wild Poppies), near Argenteuil, 1873.

Oil on canvas. H.50 ; W. 65. Etienne Moreau-Nélaton Bequest, 1906.

141

142

143

subject if ever there was one - anticipated later developments in his work.

Renoir continued his love affair with the human figure. His *Etude: torse, effet de soleil (Study Nude in the Sunlight)*, accused by hostile critics of suggesting 'a pile of decomposing flesh', shows how he pursued the study of colour to the point where the forms seem almost to dissolve in a shimmering haze of varying intensity. Nevertheless his acknowledged masterpiece of this period is *Bal du Moulin de la Galette (Dancing at the Moulin de la Galette)*, an evocation of life in Montmartre.

Pissarro (1830-1903) lived at Pontoise, north-east of Paris, and concentrated for the most part on landscapes. Like his friend Cézanne, who regularly worked with him, he was much concerned with the structure of forms. Alfred Sisley (1839–99) developed a style close to Monet's, working mainly at Louveciennes and Marly.

Two women were closely associated with the Impressionist group: Berthe Morisot (1841-99), whose painting has many points in common with that of her brother-in-law, Manet, and Mary Cassatt (1844-1926), on whom Degas was the crucial influence.

142
Mary Cassatt
Femme cousant dans un jardin, dit aussi *Jeune fille au jardin (Woman Sewing, or, Girl in Garden)*, circa 1880-1882.

Oil on canvas. H. 92 ; W. 63.
Antonin Personnaz Bequest, 1937.

143
Gustave Caillebotte
Raboteurs de parquets (Planing the Floor), 1875.

Oil on canvas. H. 102 ; W. 146.5.
Gift of Gustave Caillebotte's heirs via Auguste Renoir, his executor, 1894.

144

145

Degas

146

Edgar Degas (1834-1917) figured prominently in the first exhibition of the embryonic Impressionist group in 1874. Although his career in the 1860s had appeared to be proceeding along traditional lines, it was above all his choice of subjects from contemporary reality - the ballet, Parisian cafés, working girls, milliners and washerwomen, the races - and the Naturalism of his portraits that transformed him within the space of a few years into one of the most masterly exponents of the 'new painting'. Degas' love of unusual angles and viewpoints was accompanied by precise draughtsmanship and bold, flowing forms; his palette, which was initially dark and austere, later expanded to include a range of acid tones.

147

144
Alfred Sisley
*Le Chemin de la machine
(Machine Way),
Louveciennes,* 1873.

Oil on canvas. H. 54.5 ; W. 73.
Bequeathed in 1914 by Joanny
Peytel, who enjoyed usufruct
until 1918.

145
Alfred Sisley
*L'Inondation à Port-Marly
(Flooding at Port-Marly),*
1876.

Oil on canvas. H. 60 ; W. 81.
Isaac de Camondo Bequest, 1911.

146
Edgar Degas
Dans un café, dit aussi
L'Absinthe (At the Café, or,
Absinthe), 1876.

Oil on canvas. H. 92 ; W. 68.
Isaac de Camondo Bequest, 1911.

147
Edgar Degas
Le Défilé, dit aussi *Chevaux
de courses devant les
tribunes (Race-horses in
Front of the Stands),* circa
1866-1868.

Oil on paper on canvas.
H. 46 ; W. 61.
Isaac de Camondo Bequest, 1911.

148
Edgar Degas
L'Etoile (The Star), circa
1878.

Pastel. H. 60 ; W. 44. Gustave
Caillebotte Bequest, 1894.

149
Edgar Degas
*Les Repasseuses (Women
Ironing)*, circa 1884-1886.

Oil on canvas. H. 76 ; W. 81.5.
Isaac de Camondo Bequest, 1911.

150
Edgar Degas
*Grande Danseuse habillée
(Little Dancer of Fourteen
Years*, or, *Large Dancer,
Clothed)*,

Bronze cast from the wax
original exhibited at the sixth
Impressionist show, 1881.
H. 98 ; W. 35.2 ; D. 24.5.
Purchased in 1930 thanks to the
generosity of the artist's heirs and
the Hébrard metal foundry.

148

149

Manet

Sur la plage (On the Beach) was painted in 1873 at Berck-sur-Mer, presumably as a *plein-air* picture. It represents Manet's wife Suzanne, who frequently modelled for her husband, and his brother Eugène, shortly to marry Berthe Morisot. A work like this illustrates just how different Manet's style of painting was from that of his young Impressionist friends, even where the subject matter was analogous. Manet's vision was essentially a blend of classical and Japanese influences: the gradation of shades of grey in the foreground is worthy of Frans Hals or Velazquez. Around 1874 he painted extensively in Argenteuil, with Monet, but refused to take part in the group exhibitions of the so-called independents, continuing to submit his work to the official Salon in spite of the unrelenting hostility of the critics. Afflicted with partial paralysis in 1880, he died in 1883.

It is only fitting that the Musée d'Orsay feature a fine portrait by Manet of Georges Clemenceau (1841-1929), the politician who did so much to help the Impressionists. It was he who gave official blessing to Monet's campaign to purchase Manet's *Olympia* for the Louvre in 1907, and he also saw that Monet, in the latter years of his life, was commissioned to produce the great series of *Nymphéas (Waterlilies)* in the Orangerie.

151

152

151
Edouard Manet
Georges Clemenceau (1841-1929), 1879.

Oil on canvas. H. 94.5 ; W. 74. Gift of Mrs. Louisine W. Havemeyer, 1927.

152
Edouard Manet
Sur la plage (On the Beach, Mme Edouard Manet (1830-1906) and Eugène Manet (1833-1892), the artist's wife and brother, at Berck-sur-Mer, summer 1873.

Oil on canvas. H. 59.5 ; W. 73. Bequeathed in 1953 in memory of Jacques Doucet by his nephew Jean Edouard Dubrujeaud, who enjoyed usufruct until 1970.

Monet, Renoir,
Pissarro

153
Camille Pissarro
Jeune fille à la baguette ;
paysanne assise (Peasant
Girl with Stick), 1881.
Oil on canvas. H. 81 ; W. 64.7.
Isaac de Camondo Bequest, 1911.

For all the artists in the Impressionist group, the early 1880s were a time for taking stock, if not of crisis. Renoir had been exhibiting again at the Salon since 1878, enjoying a fair degree of success. His improved financial situation enabled him to travel, and he visited Algeria in 1881; the Musée d'Orsay possesses several major canvases from this trip, notable for their treatment of the strong southern light and for the many echoes of Delacroix. A trip to Italy later that year led him to rediscover the Renaissance masters he had admired in the Louvre as a young man, and his first-hand experience of classical antiquity, for example the paintings of Pompeii, had an undoubted influence on his own work. A new concern for drawing is apparent in two major compositions of 1883, *Danse à la ville (Dance in the City)* - the female model is Suzanne Valadon, later a painter herself and the mother of Maurice Utrillo - and *Danse à la campagne (Dance in the Country)*, where the model is Aline Charigot, later to become Renoir's wife. Renoir's palette became simpler and took on the acid tones that typify his work at this period. Yet with *Jeunes filles au piano (Young Girls at the Piano)*, the first painting by Renoir ever purchased for the nation (at Mallarmé's suggestion, in 1892), there is clear evidence of a move towards an altogether softer style and warmer colours. Renoir continued to paint relaxed and charming

153

154

155

154
Pierre-Auguste Renoir
Danse à la ville (Town Dance), 1883.

Oil on canvas. H. 180 ; W. 90.
Donated in lieu of estate duties,
1978.

155
Pierre-Auguste Renoir
Danse à la campagne (Country Dance), 1883.

Oil on canvas. H. 180 ; W. 90.
Purchased in 1979.

156

scenes, such as his favoured motif of female bathers, which found its culmination in the great composition of 1918–19, executed in the last few months of his life.

Like Renoir, Monet was active well into the twentieth century, the different stages of his artistic development being directly linked to particular motifs, which in turn were conditioned largely by his place of residence. Late in 1878 he moved to Vétheuil, a small village in the Seine valley between Paris and Rouen, and until 1891 he found his subject matter in the surrounding area, landscapes that reflected the changing seasons. When the Seine was frozen over during the harsh winter of 1879-80. he produced a sequence of paintings on this theme, several of which are in the museum's possession. The move down river to Giverny corresponded to a further development in his work. Monet had always liked to produce many different interpretations of a single motif, studying ephemeral effects of light as it altered through the day or over the different seasons of the year. Yet it was only with the *Meules (Haystacks)* that the

157   158   159

'series' became a feature of his working method. He wrote to his friend, the critic Gustave Geffroy: 'I am persisting with a series of different effects, but at this time of the year the sun sets so fast I cannot keep up with it... the further I get, the more I see that it will take a great deal of work to succeed in conveying what I want: "instantaneity", and above all the external "envelope", the same light spread overall.'

Other series were to follow, notably that based on Rouen Cathedral, which although dated 1894 was in fact painted in two bursts in 1892 and 1893; the sequence is well represented in the Musée d'Orsay by the bequest of Comte Isaac de Camondo, a collector with a passion for Monet's work, and by one canvas purchased by the state (coming to terms with Monet's reputation rather late in the day) in 1907.

Around the turn of the century Monet painted other series based on Giverny and London. At that time he often used canvases that were almost square, and this is also the format of his earliest paintings of waterlilies in his garden at Giverny, exhibited under the collective title *Bassin aux nymphéas (Waterlily Pool)*. This motif was Monet's central preoccupation throughout the latter period of his career, culminating in the vast decorative scheme for the two rooms of the Musée de l'Orangerie, opened to the public in 1927 after the painter's death, but planned by him with the assistance of his devoted friend Clemenceau.

124

160

161

157 to 161
Claude Monet
"Rouen Cathedral".

Although dated 1894, these five versions were painted in 1892 and 1893.

*Harmonie brune
(Harmony in Brown)*

Oil on canvas. H. 107 ; W. 73.
Purchased in 1907.
The four others belong to the Isaac de Camondo Bequest, 1911:

*Le Portail, Temps gris
(Portal, Overcast Weather)*

Oil on canvas.
H. 100 ; W. 65.

*Soleil matinal, harmonie
bleue (Morning Sun,
Harmony in Blue)*

Oil on canvas.
H. 91 ; W. 63.

*Effet du matin, harmonie
blanche (Morning Effect,
Harmony in White)*

Oil on canvas. H. 106 ; W. 63.

*Plein Soleil, harmonie
bleue et or (Full Sunlight,
Harmony in Blue and
Gold)*

Oil on canvas.
H. 107 ; W. 73.

Sisley's development, like Monet's, can be traced through the different motifs he adopted at various periods. After moving to Moret-sur-Loing in 1882, he worked almost exclusively on landscapes of that area. He died in 1899, too soon to experience his fame.

Pissarro was the only one of the Impressionists to take part in all the group exhibitions. His work, too, changed radically in the early 1880s. Previously a landscapist, he began to develop an interest in the human figure, embarking on a series of paintings of the peasants of Pontoise. *Jeune Fille à la baguette (Peasant Girl with Stick)* is a good example of his work in this period, combining sensitivity with solid construction; the alternation of fine brushwork and heavy impasto is evidence of his almost obsessive concern for technical experiment. Indeed it was this enthusiasm for new effects that led him to adopt the Neo-Impressionist or Divisionist theories of Seurat and Signac in 1886-87. It fairly rapidly became apparent that the application of strict rules did not suit his temperament, and he abandoned the method in favour of the more fluid handling that is typical of his late works - landscapes of Eragny-sur-Epte (where he moved in 1884) and views of Paris and Rouen.

162

Cézanne

162

Paul Cézanne
*La Femme à la cafetière
(Woman with Coffee Pot),*
circa 1890-1895.

Oil on canvas. H. 130.5 ; W. 96.5.
Gift of M. and Mme Jean-Victor
Pellerin, 1956.

163

Paul Cézanne
*L'Estaque, vue du golfe de
Marseille (L'Estaque: View
of the Bay of Marseille),*
circa 1878-1879.

Oil on canvas. H. 59.5 ; W. 73.
Gustave Caillebotte Bequest,
1894.

164

Paul Cézanne
*Les Joueurs de cartes (The
Card Players),* circa 1890-
1895.

Oil on canvas. H. 47.5 ; W. 57.
Isaac de Camondo Bequest, 1911.

The collections of the Musée d'Orsay contain many fine works by Paul Cézanne (1839-1906), well representing the diversity of themes treated by the painter and showing his evolution through the different stages of his career.

In his early years, Cézanne (born, like his friend Emile Zola, in Aix-en-Provence) was strongly influenced by Delacroix and the old masters, in particular the Venetian school; that debt is clearly indicated in works like *La Madeleine (Mary Magdalen),* of c. 1868-69, and *Pastorale (Pastoral)* of 1870. Inevitably he was torn between his Romantic inclinations, evident in *La femme étranglée (Strangled Woman),* and the Realist spirit abroad among the other painters of the day, following in Manet's wake. At the first Impressionist exhibition of 1874, two Cézanne canvases attracted a hail of abuse from public and critics alike: one was the famous *La Maison du pendu (House of the Hanged Man),* a landscape executed while the artist was staying with Dr Gachet at Auvers-sur-Oise (near Pontoise), working with Pissarro; the other was *Une Moderne Olympia (A Modern Olympia),* an interpretation of the theme treated previously by Manet in 1863. Another echo of Manet is the view of the bay of Marseille looking down from L'Estaque: 'It's like a playing card', Cézanne explained to Pissarro, recalling the effect in Manet's *Fifer.*

163

164

As well as his landscapes, and some early nudes in outdoor settings that look forward to the *Grandes Baigneuses (Great Bathers)* - a number of studies for which are in the Musée d'Orsay - the two genres that preoccupied Cézanne throughout his life were portraiture (or 'the figure' as he called it) and still-life. Possibly because he worked very slowly, possibly because of a certain shyness, he normally either painted self-portraits (two of which are in the Musée d'Orsay) or called on his family and friends to act as models, as in *Les joueurs de cartes (The Card Players)*. His wife was his favourite sitter, and his paintings of her reveal a desire to look beyond transient facial expressions and express more abiding qualities: the study of forms predominates over psychological analysis, as in *La femme à la cafetière (Woman with a Coffee Pot)*. The move in the direction of simplified volumes and geometricization of forms was to have a profound influence on the course of twentieth-century painting - as did Cézanne's abandonment of linear perspective in his late still-lifes, which paved the way for Cubism.

165
Paul Cézanne
Pommes et oranges (Apples and oranges), circa 1895-1900.

Oil on canvas. H. 74 ; W. 93.
Isaac de Camondo Bequest, 1911.

166
Paul Cézanne
Rochers près des grottes au-dessus de Château-Noir (Rocks near Château-Noir), circa 1904.

Oil on canvas. H. 65 ; W. 54.
Donated in lieu of estate duties, 1986.

165

166

Van Gogh

It was not until 1880 that Vincent van Gogh (1853-90), the son of a Dutch pastor, discovered his vocation as a painter. Before that he had worked for the art dealer Goupil in The Hague, London and Paris, and studied theology. His early paintings include dark and heavily impastoed oils of Dutch peasants which even at this early stage reveal something of the artist's troubled nature. In 1886 Van Gogh went to live in Paris, where his brother Théo cared for him with great devotion and gave him much-needed financial assistance. Théo, who also worked for Goupil, was receptive to new ideas in painting, and the extensive correspondence between the two brothers forms one of the most moving documents in the history of art. In Paris, Van Gogh came into contact with a creative world in ferment. The encounter with the Impressionists had an immediate effect on his painting; his palette lightened, and his subjects became more varied. *L'Italienne (The Italian Woman)* is one of his most vivid portraits, probably representing Agostina Segatori who ran the Paris cabaret *Le Tambourin*, which was a regular haunt of painters and artists of all kinds: the heightened complementary colours (red-green, blue-orange) and the abstract simplification of the compositional elements reinforce the vigorous and expressive brushwork that marks Van Gogh so clearly as the precursor of the Fauves.

In February 1888 the artist went to live in Arles in the South of France, intending to found an artistic community in which he would be joined by, among others, Paul Gauguin, for whom he had the greatest admiration. Gauguin arrived in October, but the dream rapidly turned to nightmare when a violent argument broke out between the two men and Van Gogh cut off his own ear in a fit of madness. This was the prelude to a complete mental breakdown, with only brief periods of remission. which led to Van Gogh's hospitalization and eventual suicide in 1890.

La chambre de Van Gogh à Arles (Van Gogh's Bedroom at Arles) of which there are three versions, was painted while Van Gogh was an inmate of the asylum at Saint-Rémy. It shows the room he had occupied at the time he painted his famous *Tournesols (Sunflowers)*. A glorious evocation of a past life, with a brilliancy of colouring and dizzying perspective that are in marked contrast to the orderliness of the modest room, this canvas clearly represents some sort of attempt at exorcism, for

167
Vincent Van Gogh
La Chambre de Van Gogh à Arles (Van Gogh's Bedroom at Arles), painted at Saint-Rémy, 1889.

Oil on canvas. H. 57.5 ; W. 74. Formerly in the Matsukata collection; entered the French national collection in 1969 under the terms of the peace treaty with Japan.

167

168

169

170

there can be little doubt that painting served Van Gogh as a form of personal therapy.

That cathartic mechanism is seen most clearly at work in the self-portraits, some forty in all, in which Van Gogh explored his own image, often distorted by hallucinations - as in the example, painted in 1889, in the Musée d'Orsay. The classic representative of the 'doomed artist' beloved of the nineteenth century, Van Gogh prefigured such painters of pure expression as Edvard Munch, Alexei Jawlensky and Oskar Kokoschka, who regarded art essentially as the process of projecting an inner world. This particular self-portrait was presented by Van Gogh to Dr Gachet, who was both a gifted medical practitioner - with a particular interest in mental illness - and also the friend and patron of numerous painters including Renoir, Pissarro, Cézanne and Guillaumin, all of whom stayed with him at Auvers-sur-Oise. It was to his house that Van Gogh went in May 1890 to convalesce after his latest attack, and it was there that he painted, in the little time left to him, the famous *Eglise d'Auvers (The Church at Auvers)*, an extraordinary marriage of brushwork and colour that reveals Van Gogh as the precursor of European Expressionism.

One of the conditions imposed by Dr Gachet's children was that the paintings from his distinguished collection should be grouped together; their wishes in this matter have been respected in the hanging scheme adopted in the Musée d'Orsay.

168
Vincent Van Gogh
L'Italienne (The Italian Woman), painted in Paris, 1887.

Oil on canvas. H. 81 ; W. 60. Baroness Eva Gebhard-Gourgaud Bequest, 1965.

169
Vincent Van Gogh
Portrait de l'artiste (Self-Portrait), 1889.

Oil on canvas. H. 65 ; W. 54.5. Gift of Paul and Marguerite Gachet, 1949.

170
Vincent Van Gogh
Le Docteur Paul Gachet (Portrait of Dr Gachet), painted at Auvers-sur-Oise, June 1890.

Oil on canvas. H. 68 ; W. 57. Gift of Paul and Marguerite Gachet, 1949.

171
Vincent Van Gogh
L'Eglise d'Auvers-sur-Oise, vue du chevet (Apse of the Church at Auvers-sur-Oise), June 1890.

Oil on canvas. H. 94 ; W. 74.5. Purchased with the aid of Paul Gachet and an anonymous Canadian bequest, 1951.

172

Seurat and
Néo-impressionism

173

172
Georges Seurat
Le Cirque (The Circus),
1891.

Oil on canvas. H. 185.5 ; W. 152.5.
John Quinn Bequest, 1924.

173 to 175
Georges Seurat
Les Poseuses (The Models),
three sketches, 1886-1887.

Oil on wood. H. 25 ; W. 16 ;
H. 25 ; W. 16 ; H. 24.5 ; W. 15.5.
Purchased in 1947.

In the course of a brief but intensely active career Georges Seurat (1859-91) produced a small number of masterpieces, now largely dispersed in foreign museums. The result is that Seurat is relatively little known in his own country. *Une baignade, Asnières (Bathers at Asnières)*, of 1883-84, rejected by the Salon jury and exhibited at the first Salon of the Société des Artistes Indépendants in 1884, is now in London. *Un dimanche après-midi à l'Ile de la Grande Jatte (Sunday on the Island of La Grande Jatte)*, shown at the eighth and last Impressionist exhibition of 1886, is in Chicago. *Les poseuses (The Models)*, of 1886-88, is in the Barnes Foundation, Merion, Pa. The first two of these masterpieces are represented in the Musée d'Orsay by a few working sketches, the third by a number of more finished and meticulously executed studies. Otherwise, the only examples in the museum of his perfected technique, generally known as Neo-Impressionism, are one landscape, *Port-en-Bessin* (1888), and his last painting, *Le cirque (The Circus)*, of 1891. His method consisted in the application on the canvas of tiny dabs of pure, divided colour, according to a system of formal composition founded in the equilibrium of opposites, probably based on the Golden Section. In the course of a traditional classical training, Seurat had become interested in theories of line and colour, which he studied in the writings of Blanc, Rood and Chevreul, and later with his contemporary Charles Henry. Seurat hoped to found a new 'great tradition' that would build on the achievements of Impressionism, one based on his own interpretation of modernity as extending beyond subject matter to encompass rigourous 'scientific' method. In *The Circus* - not without wit - he uses the symbolism of colour and ascendant lines to convey a sense of animated movement and celebration.

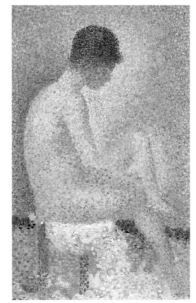

174

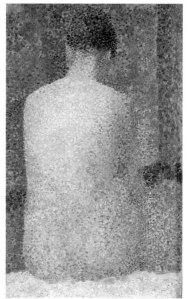

175

176

177

Seurat's theories were taken up and developed by his friend Paul Signac (1863-1935) in a manifesto published at the end of the century, *From Delacroix to Neo-Impressionism*. After Seurat's early death it fell to Signac to become leader of the movement, and he developed a method that relied more on colour and broader brushstrokes. From the late 1890s onwards he concentrated increasingly on seascapes which, in their alliance of a true Impressionist sensibility with disciplined technique, have surprising affinities with French landscapes of the seventeenth and eighteenth centuries. Of the other members of the group, which held together until the mid 1890s (Charles Angrand, Maximilien Luce, Albert Dubois-Pillet, and for a time Camille Pissarro and Théo van Rysselberghe, among others), it was Henri-Edmond Cross (1856–1910) who, alongside Signac, remained loyal to Seurat's technique for the rest of his life. His *L'air du soir (Evening Breeze)*, though Neo-Impressionist or 'Divisionist' in manner, demonstrates a fine aesthetic sense that is typical of the *fin de siècle* and somewhat reminiscent of the Nabis, Maurice Denis in particular.

178

Toulouse-Lautrec

179
Henri de Toulouse-Lautrec
*Henry Samary, de la
Comédie-Française, dans
le rôle de Raoul de Vaubert
dans la comédie de
J. Sandeau, Mademoiselle
de La Seiglière (Henry
Samary Performing at the
Comédie Française)*, 1889.

Oil on cardboard. H. 75 ; W. 52.
Bequeathed in 1947 by Jacques
Laroche, who enjoyed usufruct
until 1976.

180
Henri de Toulouse-Lautrec
La Toilette (Washing), 1896.

Oil on cardboard. H. 65 ; W. 54.
Pierre Goujon Bequest, 1914.

orn of an aristocratic family from south-west France, Henri de Toulouse-Lautrec (1864-1901) suffered in his youth a series of accidents that left him permanently disabled. It was the combination of piercing intelligence with physical deformity that created one of the most eccentric personalities of the *fin de siècle*, a man who could be intensely touching or woundingly sarcastic. Compensating for his infirmities by emancipating himself from bourgeois convention, Lautrec plunged into the nocturnal world of Paris theatres, clubs and brothels, finding there the models for his paintings, which are markedly influenced by Degas and Japanese prints. In true Baudelairian spirit, he sought beauty in degradation, and his oils, pastels and lithographs provide an exceptionally vivid picture of the world of entertainment in the late nineteenth century.

In 1895 the dancer La Goulue, formerly a celebrity of the Moulin Rouge, asked the artist to decorate a fairground booth at the Foire du Trône where she planned to present her new act. Lautrec was inspired to produce two large canvases in which he invested all his skill as a poster artist, one showing La Goulue dancing at the Moulin Rouge with her partner "Valentin the Double-Jointed", the other representing her as a Moorish dancer.

Women – whether actresses, society ladies or prostitutes – were the principal source of Lautrec's inspiration, as seen in *La Toilette* of 1896 and the album of lithographs, *Elles*, published in the same year.

179

180

181 and 182
Henri de Toulouse-Lautrec
*La Danse au Moulin
Rouge, La Goulue et
Valentin le désossé
(Dancing at the Moulin-
Rouge, La Goulue and
"Valentin the Double-
Jointed")* et
La Danse mauresque ou
*La Goulue en almée (The
Moorish Dance or La
Goulue as a Moorish
Dancer)*,
Panels decorating La Goulue's
booth at the Foire du Trône 1895.

Oil on canvas. H. 298 ; W. 316 ;
H. 285 ; W. 307.5.
Purchased in fragments, in 1929,
with the exception of the section
showing Valentin le Désossé,
donated by Monsieur Auffray,
1929; restored 1930.

Redon

183
Odilon Redon
Le Bouddha (Buddha),
circa 1905.

Pastel. H. 90 ; W. 73.
Purchased in 1971.

184
Odilon Redon
*Les Yeux clos (Eyes
Closed),* 1890.

Oil on canvas on cardboard.
H. 44 ; W. 36. Purchased in 1904.

Working largely in isolation, Odilon Redon (1840-1916) produced a body of work of striking originality. Derived almost entirely from the unconscious and dreams, his pictures are peopled with mysterious creatures, gnomes and fantastic animals and flowers. Together with Puvis de Chavannes and Gustave Moreau, he is one of the principal representatives of French Symbolism.

Redon's early work is largely in black-and-white (charcoal drawings and lithographs) and, like the rest of his oeuvre, is often inspired by literature (Poe, Flaubert, etc.). His externalization of private fantasies is entirely characteristic of the climate that prevailed in *the fin-de-siècle* years, and of the vein of lyrical introspection that ran through French poetry from Baudelaire to Mallarmé. In 1890 Redon began to experiment with colour, still using the same subject matter. *Les yeux clos (Closed Eyes)* was the first of his works to be acquired for the nation. Ultimately it was pastel that provided Redon with the sumptuous effects best suited to convey his fantastic imagery. His virtuoso use of the medium is unsurpassed, as witness *Le Bouddha (Buddha),* one of the most famous of the many pastels by him in the Musée d'Orsay (a collection assembled for the most part from the gifts and bequests of the artist's widow Suzanne and son Arï, and from donations by Claude Roger-Marx).

184

185

185
Paul Gauguin
Self-portrait with Yellow Christ, 1889-1890.

Oil on canvas. H. 38 ; W. 46. Purchased in 1994 with the aid of Philippe Meyer and Japanese contributions organized by the daily paper *Nikkei*.

Of the many Gauguin self-portraits, this is probably one of the most authentic. Rather than cultivating the image of *artiste maudit* ("accursed artist") in this painting done in Brittany during a difficult period, Gauguin here explores a personal symbolism of self-interrogation that underscores his own conflicting aspirations.

The Pont-Aven School

Pont-Aven is a Breton village near Concarneau where a number of artists congregated, united in their desire to emphasize their differences from Impressionism. Gauguin went there in 1888. Emile Bernard (1868-1941), who arrived in August 1888, became the group's theorist: 'Synthetism' and 'simplification' are the key-words he noted down on the back of his *Nature morte au pot de grès (Still-life with Stoneware Pot)*, in the Musée d'Orsay. For the portrait of his sister Madeleine reclining in the Bois d'Amour at Pont-Aven, he adopted a downward perspective and outlined the flat areas of colour in black. It was a lesson effortlessly absorbed by Paul Sérusier (1863–1927), who also worked at Pont-Aven. On the back of one of his pictures he noted that it was painted 'in October 1888 under Gauguin's guidance': this landscape, without perspective, dominated by intense, pure tones of colour, was to become the famous *Talisman* of the Nabis (see p. 137).

Other painters such as Charles Laval (1862-94) and Charles Filiger (1863-1928) seized on these simple motifs, and Brittany came to represent, for them and many others, the mystic innocence of a primitive society.

186

187

Gauguin

Paul Gauguin (1848-1903) began painting as an amateur, and it was due to his success at the Impressionists' group exhibitions, in which he participated from 1880 onwards, that he decided to become a full-time painter.

Pont-Aven in Brittany was the first port of call in a journey of discovery that was to last a lifetime. Gauguin stayed there in 1887, 1888, 1889-90, and again in 1894, associating with the painters who have come to be known collectively as the Pont-Aven School, some of whom were manifestly influenced by him.

In between trips to Brittany, Gauguin also travelled to Martinique, paid a brief visit to Van Gogh in Arles, and spent time in Paris. *La belle Angèle*, of 1889, is a good illustration of Gaugin's distinctive synthesis of *Cloisonnisme* (the use of black outlines) and Symbolism, incorporating Japanese influences and a feeling for decorative simplicity inherited from Puvis de Chavannes. It expresses, too, the love of the primitive world that took him to Tahiti for the first time in 1891-93. There Gauguin found the themes and the spiritual significance his work demanded, and he developed an interest in the native religions and crafts that powerfully influenced the nature of his later sculptures.

His return to France in 1893 proved to be no more than an interlude, and in 1895 he left again for Polynesia, where he died in 1903.

188
Paul Gauguin
La Belle Angèle (Fair Angela), 1889.
Oil on canvas. H. 92 ; W. 73.
Gift of Ambroise Vollard, 1927.

189
Paul Gauguin
Le Repas (The Meal), 1891.
Oil on canvas. H. 73 ; W. 92.
Bequeathed in 1954 by M. and Mme André Meyer, who enjoyed usufruct until 1975.

190
Paul Gauguin
Le Cheval blanc (The White Horse), 1898.
Oil on canvas. H. 140 ; W. 91.5.
Purchased in 1927.

188

189

Sculpture:
Gauguin and the Nabis

Following on from a brief experiment with ceramics in 1886–87, Gauguin produced a number of painted wooden sculptures, among them a relief called *Soyez mystérieuses (Be Mysterious)*, on which he worked at Le Pouldu, in Brittany, in 1890. The style he adopted - polychrome effects, simplified forms with flattened planes and areas of contrasting shadow - was influenced by his acquaintance with Breton folk art and the so-called primitive arts in general. His distinctive combination of modelling, colour and abbreviated formal construction transforms these works from representational objects into archaic emblems.

An artist who shared Gauguin's appreciation of pagan idols was Georges Lacombe (1868-1916), introduced to the Nabi group by Sérusier. His *Danses bretonnes (Breton Dances)* of 1894 is a subtle combination of flat colour with fluid line; similarly, he was able to blend sophisticated technique with primitivism in transforming a carved bed into a symbol of the mystery of human life. Another life-cycle emblem is his *Isis*, showing the goddess squeezing her breasts to issue two streams of blood, representing the life force. The freedom and spontaneity of this type of direct sculpture is reflected in its bold polychrome effects, expressive deformations and accentuated physical characteristics.

191

191
Paul Gauguin
La Maison du Jouir (House of Bliss), 1901.

Painted sequoia wood.
Purchased in 1952 and in 1990.
Decorative panelling around the door to Gauguin's cabin at
Atuana on Hiva-oa Island.

192

192
Paul Gauguin
Idole à la perle (Idol with Pearl), circa 1892-1893.

Wood. H. 23.7. W. 12.6. D. 11.4.
Donated in 1951 by Mme Huc de
Monfreid, who enjoyed usufruct
until 1968.

A stroke of luck in 1990 enabled the Musée d'Orsay to acquire the missing fifth panel of entrance decoration to Gaugin's *Maison du Jouir (House of Bliss)*, the other four panels of which had been acquired in 1952. Delicate colouring, softened by age, enhances the naive yet sensuous charm of the figures. The trace of the artist's hand remain visible everywhere, his toolmarks in bare wood giving a deliberately rustic feel to the carving.

193

Paul Gauguin
Idole à la coquille (Idol with Shell), 1893.

Wood. H. 34.4. ; W. 14.8. ; D. 18.5.
Donated in 1951 by Mme Huc de Monfreid, who enjoyed usufruct until 1968.

194

Georges Lacombe
L'Existence (Existence), 1892.

Wood, headboard of bed from the Nabis' studio.
H. 68.5 ; W. 41.5 ; D. 6.
Purchased in 1956.

193

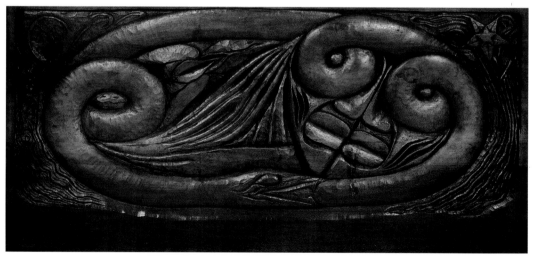

194

195

195
Paul Gauguin
Soyez mystérieuses (Be Mysterious), 1890.

Painted wood.
H. 73 ; W. 95 ; D. 5.
Purchased in 1978.

196
Georges Lacombe
Isis, circa 1893-1894.

Painted wood.
H. 111.5 ; W. 62 ; D. 10.7.
Purchased in 1982.

196

The Nabis

197
Pierre Bonnard
La Partie de croquet ou
*Le Crépuscule (The Game
of Croquet,* or, *Twilight),*
1892.

Oil on canvas. H. 130 ; W. 162.5.
Gift of Daniel Wildenstein via the
Société des Amis d'Orsay, 1985.

198
Edouard Vuillard
*Femme de profil au
chapeau vert (Profile of
Woman in Green Hat),*
circa 1891.

Oil on cardboard. H. 21 ; W. 16.
Donated in lieu of estate duties,
1990.

198

The Nabis did not in the strict sense constitute a school; rather they were a group of painters who were friends and who between 1888 and 1900 shared a common desire to breathe new life into painting. The members of the original group were Pierre Bonnard (1867-1947), Edouard Vuillard (1868–1940), Maurice Denis (1870–1943), Ker-Xavier Roussel (1867-1944) and Paul Ranson (1864-1909), who were students together at the Académie Julian and the Ecole des Beaux-Arts, joined soon afterwards by Félix Vallotton (1865–1925), of Swiss origin, and the sculptor Aristide Maillol (1861–1944). Their hero was Gauguin, whose famous watchword 'the freedom to dare all' was passed on to them by Sérusier on the fateful day in October 1888 when he showed them his *Talisman*, painted under Gauguin's guidance. They also admired Puvis de Chavannes, Redon and Cézanne. Denis painted a *Hommage à Cézanne (Homage to Cézanne)*, now in the Musée d'Orsay, which shows the members of the Nabi group.

The young men regarded themselves as prophets of a new painting; the Hebrew word *nabi* means 'prophet'. Admiring Japanese prints, they copied their simplified forms, flat colour and lack of depth. Thus Bonnard, dubbed by his fellows *'le nabi japonard'*, treats the members of his family in his *Partie de croquet (The Game of Croquet)*, as silhouettes standing out sharply against a background composed of a series of large decorative masses.

As a group, they wanted to get away from easel painting and therefore tended to look to the arts of décor, from theatre design to paintings for domestic interiors, a field in which their talents flourished. The Musée d'Orsay possesses five of the nine panels painted by Vuillard in 1894 for Alexandre Natanson, editor of the famous *Revue blanche*, who commissioned the sequence for his Paris flat on the avenue du Bois, now avenue Foch. In this decorative scheme, spatial depth is conveyed by a rhythmic interpenetration of planes suggested, perhaps, by no more than the vertical of a tree-trunk or the curved outline of a clump of trees. The same rhythmic composition is apparent in Maurice

199
Félix Vallotton
Le Ballon (The Ball), 1899.

Oil on cardboard on wood.
H. 48 ; W. 61.
Carle Dreyfus Bequest, 1953.

200 and 201
Edouard Vuillard
Jardins publics (The Park),
five of nine decorative panels
executed for Alexandre
Natanson, 1894.

Left to right:
*Les Fillettes jouant (Girls
Playing)*
Oil on canvas. H. 214.5 ; W. 88.
*L'Interrogatoire (The
Interrogation)*
Oil on canvas. H. 214.5 ; W. 92.
Radot Bequest, 1978.
*La Conversation (The
Conversation)*
Oil on canvas. H. 213 ; W. 154.
Les Nourrices (Nannies)
Oil on canvas. H. 213.5 ; 73.
*L'Ombrelle rouge (The Red
Parasol)*
Oil on canvas. H. 214 ; W. 81.
Purchased in 1929 and bequest of
Mme Alexandre Radot, 1978.

202

202
Maurice Denis
Les Muses (The Muses),
1893.

Oil on canvas. H. 171.5 ; W. 137.5.
Purchased in 1932.

201

Denis's modern interpretation of the mythological *Muses*, very much in the spirit of Art Nouveau with its emphasis on such decorative elements as the leaves of the chestnut trees and the generous deployment of serpentine curves.

Vallotton made eloquent use of foreshortening, influenced by his experience of wood-engraving, and conveyed a sense of space by the juxtaposition of dark and light areas, set in a rising, horizonless perspective.

It is this free handling of motifs, often accompanied by marvellously subtle distortions, this fundamentally decorative approach, that makes the Nabi movement so significant in the development of painting towards autonomy, one of the mainsprings of modern art.

203
Aristide Maillol
Danseuse (Dancer), 1895.
Wood. H. 22 ; W. 24.5 ; D. 5.
Mme Thadée Natanson Bequest, 1953.

204
Ker-Xavier Roussel
La terrasse (The Terrace), circa 1892.
Oil on canvas. H. 36 ; W. 75.
Purchased in 1992.

205
Maurice Denis
*L'enfant au pantalon bleu
(Child in Blue Trousers),*
1897.

Oil on canvas. H. 52.5 ; W. 39.2.
Purchased in 1987.

205

206

206
Pierre Bonnard
Intimité (Privacy), 1891.

Oil on canvas. H. 28 ; W. 36.
Purchased with the aid of
Philippe Meyer in 1992.

Douanier Rousseau

207
Henri ('Le Douanier')
Rousseau
*La Charmeuse de serpents
(The Snake Charmer)*, 1907.
Oil on canvas. H. 169 ; W. 189.5.
Jacques Doucet Bequest, 1936.

Although of the same generation as the major Impressionists, Henri Rousseau (1844-1910), born at Laval, stands quite apart from the mainstream of art at the turn of the century. He worked as a toll-collector in Paris - hence the nickname *Douanier* or 'customs-officer' and was initially an amateur painter. Self-taught, he used to copy the Old Masters in the Louvre, and proclaimed his admiration for the great academic painters of the period, such as Gérôme. The circumstances of his life were otherwise quite ordinary, and the man remains as much of an enigma as the works he produced, the modernity of which disconcerted not a few of his contemporaries.

With encouragement from Signac, he exhibited at the Salon des Indépendants in 1880, and continued to do so right up to his death; he was also represented at the Salon d'Automne of 1905, where the Fauves made their explosive entry onto the artistic scene.

Rousseau created a strange world often overlaid with symbolic references, as in *La guerre (War)* of 1894, in the Musée d'Orsay, which contains echoes of the Italian Primitives. He took liberties with form, as his imagination dictated; compositional audacities such as his have been quite consciously cultivated by modern artists. No doubt it was for reasons such as these that poets and painters of the avant-garde sought him out, among them Jarry, Apollinaire, Delaunay and Picasso - whose collection of Rousseau's pictures is now in the Musée Picasso in Paris.

As well as many portraits, landscapes and historical scenes, painted in a style of deceptive naivety, Rousseau also produced a jungle series: beasts of prey attacking antelopes or staring out at the onlooker, surrounded by luxuriant tropical vegetation (which Rousseau modelled on plants he had seen in the Botanical Gardens in Paris). His fabulous exoticism is essentially a framework for an exuberant decorative impulse of great power and charm. This is particularly true of works such as *Charmeuse de serpents (The Snake Charmer)*, a mythical Eden painted in 1907 for the mother of the painter Robert Delaunay.

Drawing and
Watercolour

From youthful iconoclasts to upholders of academicism, practically all the artists active between 1870 and the end of the century did a great deal of drawing, employing the whole range of established techniques. Thus the tradition of Ingres lived on, not only among the ranks of official painters but through Puvis de Chavannes, Degas, Seurat and Renoir, to mention but a few of those whose graphic work figures extensively in the collections.

Boudin, whose pastels and watercolours were praised by Baudelaire, is represented here by a superb series of small-scale studies. The Impressionists (notably Pissarro) all practised drawing, as did their precursor Manet and their immediate

208
Georges Seurat
La Voilette (The Half Veil),
circa 1883.

Conté crayon. H. 31.5 ; W. 24.2.
Donated in lieu of estate duties,
1982.

208

209

209
Georges Seurat
Le nœud noir (The Black Bow), circa 1882.
Conté crayon. H. 31 ; W. 23.
Purchased in 1989.

210

211

210
Paul Gauguin
Noa-Noa (fol. 75), 1893-1897.

Pen and black ink, India ink,
wash of India ink and
watercolour. H. 30.4 ; W. 28.8.
Gift of Daniel de Monfreid, 1927.

211
Paul Cézanne
*Nature morte avec
grenades, carafe, sucrier,
bouteille et pastèque (Still-
life with Pomegranates,
Carafe, Sugar-bowl, Bottle
and Water Melon)*, circa
1900-1906.

Watercolour. H. 31.5 ; W. 43.2.
Donated in lieu of estate duties,
1982.

212

212
Edgar Degas
*Chez la modiste (At the
Milliner's)*, circa 1905-1910.
Pastel on paper. H. 91 ; W. 75.
Purchased in 1979.

213
Edgar Degas
Le tub (The Tub), 1886.
Pastel on cardboard.
H. 60 ; W. 83.
Isaac de Camondo Bequest.

213

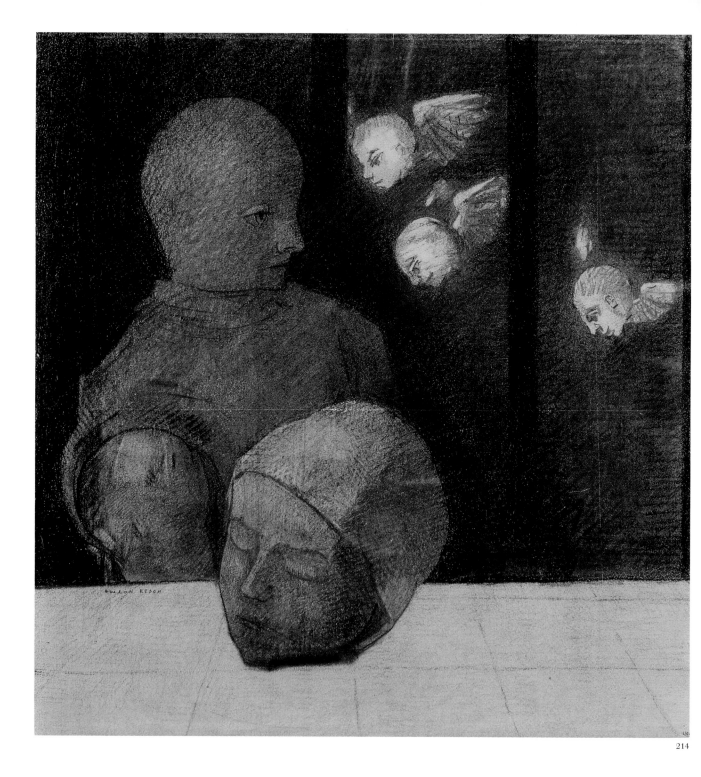

successors. If Degas was the master in the use of pastel, there were many others, notably Mary Cassatt, who also made brilliant use of the medium. It was adopted to great effect by Redon, who in the early part of his career was known as the master of black-and-white. Nor should one forget Cézanne's watercolours, with their transparent ordered masses, a major element of his oeuvre, or the watercolours of a very different style executed by Signac and his Neo-Impressionist friends.

It is perhaps Gauguin who makes the most impressive contribution, with his manuscript *Noa-Noa*, written in collaboration with Charles Morice and illustrated with watercolours and colour engravings, together with various other figures and photographs; based on Gauguin's reminiscences of his first visit to Tahiti, the book is a living testament to all that the painter held most dear.

214
Odilon Redon
Le Prisonnier (The Prisoner), circa 1880.
Charcoal on buff paper.
H. 39.5 ; W. 37. Claude Roger-Marx Bequest, 1974.

215

216

215
Henri Gervex
Landscape (Dieppe), circa
1885.

Pastel. H. 60 ; W. 30.
Purchased in 1988.

216
Ker-Xavier Roussel
La barrière (The Gate),
circa 1891-1893.

Pastel on paper. H. 21.5 ; W. 17.
Purchased in 1991.

163

Photography

Spreading through advanced artistic organizations at the turn of the century - notably in the English-speaking countries - the movement towards 'art' or 'pictorialist' photography marked a decisive stage in the realization of the creative potential of the medium. It established the validity of the photographer's subjective vision and legitimized the role of imagination in photography. Pride of place is therefore given in the museum displays to this type of photography, which is closely related to the aesthetics of Art Nouveau and the paintings of the Impressionists, Symbolists and Nabis exhibited elsewhere in the collections.

It was in England, as photographers began to draw on literary and Romantic sources in the composition of their works, that the debate raged most fiercely over whether photographs could ever equal painting. Julia Margaret Cameron (1815-79) succeeded in revolutionizing the whole concept of portrait photography. Using purely photographic means (close-up and soft-focus) she anticipated certain effects of film in her timeless transpositions of scenes from Italian Renaissance painting. Cameron's innovations (though not her Italianate subjects) were assimilated in the work of Edward Steichen (1879-1973), one of the members of the American Photo-Secession group founded in 1902 by Alfred Stieglitz (1864-1946), himself one of

217
Frederick Henry Evans
The Illustrator Aubrey Beardsley (1872-1898),
1894.

Platinotype. H. 15 ; W. 10.
Purchased in 1985.

218
Julia Margaret Cameron
Maud (illustration for
The Idylls of the King and Other Poems by Tennyson,
variant), 1874-1875.

Carbon print. H. 33.2 ; W. 28.
Purchased in 1985.

217

218

219

219
Paul Burty-Haviland
Woman in Kimono at Rest.
Cyanotype print.
H. 20.3 ; W. 25.4.
Purchased in 1993.

the great portrait photographers. *The Kiss* by Clarence White (1871-1925), another member of the group, takes its inspiration directly from the illustrations of Aubrey Beardsley and the paintings of the pre-Raphaelites. In contrast Stieglitz's series *City of Ambition* presents a wonderfully vivid symbolic portrait of New York. His shot of immigrants travelling steerage, of 1907 - an image admired by Picasso - marks the definitive emergence of a new photography.

220

220
Edward Steichen
The Artist and his Wife on Honeymoon at Lake George, 1903.
Platinotype and glycerine.
H. 21 ; W. 25. Purchased in 1982.

221
Edgar Degas
Portrait of Madame Ludovic Halévy, née Louise Breguet, circa 1895.
Silver gelatin print.
H. 40.6 ; W. 29.3. Gift of the children of Mme Halévy-Joxe, 1994.

222
Edgar Degas
Portrait of Daniel Halévy, circa 1895.
Silver gelatin print. H. 40.7 ; W. 29.7. Gift of the children of Mme Halévy-Joxe, 1994.

221

222

224

223

223
Alfred Stieglitz
The Steerage, 1907.

Printed by photogravure on
Japan paper in 1915 for the
review 291.
H. 19.7 ; W. 16.
Purchased in 1984.

224
Alfred Stieglitz
City of Ambition, 1910.

Printed by photogravure on
Japan paper, 1910-1915.
H. 33.7 ; W. 25.9. Purchased in
1980.

225
Clarence Hudson White
The Kiss, 1904.

Platinotype, gelatin treated with
bichromate. H. 24.5 ; W. 14.7.
Gift of the Société CdF Chimie
Terpolymères, 1985.

225

Art and Decoration
in the Third Republic

226
Ernest Barrias
*La Nature se dévoilant à la
Science (Nature Unveiling
Herself to Science)*, 1899.

Marble, onyx, malachite, lapis
lazuli, granite.
H. 200 ; W. 85 ; D. 55.
Commissioned for the
Conservatoire des Arts et Métiers
in 1899, entered the national
collections in 1903.

227
Jean-Léon Gérôme
Tanagra, 1890.

Polychrome marble.
H. 154.7 ; W. 56 ; D. 57.3.
Purchased in 1890.

227

The Third Republic (which lasted from 1870 to 1940) sought to demonstrate its permanence and stability by erecting monuments to its glory. In 1879 the Paris municipal authorities held a competition which resulted in the construction of Charles Morice's monument in the place de la République, and the *Triomphe de la République (The Triumph of the Republic)* by Jules Dalou (1838–1902) in the place de la Nation. When the statesman Léon Gambetta died, in 1882, the moment was seized upon to celebrate his achievements in defending France and founding the Republic. A competition was held - this was thought to be the most democratic method - for a design to be financed by public subscription. The winners were the architect Louis-Charles Boileau and the sculptor Jean-Paul Aubé, who chose a site on the Cour Napoléon, facing the Second Empire portion of the Louvre. From the first, the 36-foot-high memorial attracted criticism. The bronzes were melted down during the German Occupation, and the stonework was removed in 1954. The remaining part of the central group was re-erected behind the *mairie* of the 20th arrondissement in Paris to commemorate the centenary of Gambetta's death, but it gives a very incomplete idea of the symbolic and didactic scheme of the original. The model which won the competition has been restored for the Musée d'Orsay; it is highly typical of a type of monument that remained in vogue up to the early years of the twentieth century. Aubé also provided the model for a magnificent table centrepiece appropriate to the sumptuous and leisurely banquets of a bygone age.

Science was one of the cornerstones of the Republic, and Ernest Barrias's weighty allegory of *La Nature se dévoilant à la Science (Nature Unveiling Herself to Science)* was intended to reflect the positivist certainties of the times. The beauty of the onyx, malachite and lapis lazuli in itself provides a potent - if unintended - metaphor of the understanding of the material world.

The Third Republic relied heavily on popular celebrations to inspire and unite its citizens. The 14th of July was decreed a national holiday in 1880, and the World Fairs of 1878, 1889 and 1900 were accompanied by festivities on a massive scale. Just as the Counter-Reformation favoured the rise of the Baroque, so the Republic engendered a sculptural style that was exuberant and full of animation. Alexandre Falguière (1831-1900) produced just such a design for a sculptural group to crown the Arc de Triomphe. The wax model was displayed at the exhibition of decorative arts held in 1882, and a commission was extended for a full-scale plaster cast the quadriga seen in photographs of Victor Hugo's funeral. However, the final commission was never issued, and the model remains virtually the only record of the many projects that were considered during the nineteenth century to crown the Arc de Triomphe.

229

228
Jules Coutan
Les Chasseurs d'aigles (The Eagle Hunters), 1900.

Plaster. H. 5.35 ; W. 305 ; D. 120. Model for bronze commissioned 1893 for the palaeontology gallery of the Muséum d'Histoire Naturelle by the architect Dutert.

229
Jean-Baptiste-Paul Cabet
Mil huit cent soixante et onze (Eighteen Hundred Seventy-One).

Marble. H. 125 ; W. 66 ; D. 101. Commissioned by the nation in 1873.

230
Gustave Deloye
Saint Marc (St Mark), 1878.

Plaster. H. 205 ; W. 143 ; D. 120. Purchased in 1878.

231
Emmanuel Fremiet
Jeanne d'Arc (Joan of Arc), 1872-1874.

Plaster. H. 75 ; W. 46 ; D. 22. Scale model of the first equestrian statue at Place des Pyramides in Paris. Donated in 1979 by Mme Fauré-Fremiet, who enjoyed usufruct until 1984.

Gustave Deloye (1838-99), who had travelled in Central Europe, made use of a similarly theatrical style for his group of *Saint Marc sur le lion (St Mark on the Lion).* Emanuel Fremiet (1824-1910) aligned himself with this vigorous trend when he created the Pegasuses which take wing on the north pylons of the Pont Alexandre III - although his true vocation was for historical Realism. The replica of his *Saint Michel (St Michael),* on the Mont-Saint Michel, is a massive work in beaten copper by the firm of Monduit, over 20 feet high; in spite of the scale, the armour is faithfully reproduced in every detail, as is that of his famous *Jeanne d'Arc (Joan of Arc)* in the place des Pyramides in Paris, commissioned in 1872. In response to criticisms that the horse was wrongly proportioned for its rider, the sculptor actually replaced the original statue with a new one in 1899, at his own expense.

230

231

The political upheavals of 1870-71 - the Franco-Prussian War, the Commune, the installation of the Third Republic could hardly fail to find some reflection in the artistic sphere. Works directly inspired by political events were, however, slow to emerge. Even *L'énigme (The Enigma)* by Gustave Doré (1832-83), painted in 1871 (as were two other compositions explicitly citing the German eagle), was in fact a response to some lines written long before by Victor Hugo:

O Spectacle. Ainsi meurt ce que les peuples font!
Qu'un tel passé pour l'âme est un gouffre profond
O spectacle. Thus do the deeds of peoples die !
How deep an abyss, for the soul, is such a past !

These particular pictures remained in the artist's studio, and were not seen in public until the posthumous auction of Doré's work.

The old styles of painting suffered scarcely a setback. Jules (1836-1911) was a painter in the full academic tradition, and winner of the Prix de Rome in 1861. His *Vérité (Truth)* was exhibited at the Salon of 1870, purchased for the nation and installed in the Musée du Luxembourg in 1874, the year of the Impressionists' first exhibition.

A few years later the state severed its links with the official Salon, handing over responsibility for the selection process to the Société des Artistes Français in 1880. And yet official art continued to flourish. The reason is not hard to seek. Lefebvre and Bouguereau, for example, were teachers at the Académie Julian. It was they, and others of the same persuasion, who formed and modelled the younger generation of artists.

232
Jean-Paul Laurens
L'Excommunication de Robert le Pieux (The Excommunication of Robert the Pious), 1875.
Oil on canvas. H. 130 ; W. 218.
Purchased in 1875.

233

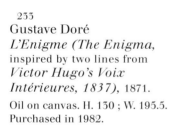

233
Gustave Doré
L'Enigme (The Enigma,
inspired by two lines from
*Victor Hugo's Voix
Intérieures, 1837),* 1871.

Oil on canvas. H. 130 ; W. 195.5.
Purchased in 1982.

234
Jules Lefebvre
La Vérité (Truth), Salon of
1870.

Oil on canvas. H. 264.7 ; W. 111.8.
Purchased in 1871.

234

255

255
Fernand Cormon
Caïn (Cain, inspired by the
opening lines of "Conscience",
from *Victor Hugo's* La
Légende des Siècles,
1859), Salon of 1880.

Oil on canvas. H. 380 ; W. 700.
Purchased in 1880.

256
Jules Bastien-Lepage
Les Foins (Haymaking),
1877.

Oil on canvas. H. 160 ; W. 195.
Purchased in 1885.

236

237

237
Emmanuel Fremiet
*Saint Michel terrassant le
dragon (St. Michael
Slaying the Dragon)*, 1879-
1896.
Beaten copper (executed by the
Monduit firm).
H. 617 ; W. 260 ; D. 120.
Gift of Mme G. Pasquier to the
Monuments Historiques, on
permanent loan from the
Direction du Patrimoine, 1980.
Replica of the statue crowning
the spire of Mont-Saint-Michel in
Brittany.

The history painter Jean-Paul Laurens (1838-1921) experienced his hour of glory in the early years of the Third Republic, specializing in patriotic themes which - like *L'excommunication de Robert le Pieux (The Excommunication of Robert the Pious)* of 1875 - were reproduced in school textbooks.

The younger artists were not entirely oblivious of the new Naturalism. One of the big successes of the Salon of 1880 was *Caïn (Cain)*, an ambitious composition by Fernand Cormon (1845-1924) that dispensed entirely with the smooth-surfaced academic manner, while still being based on preparatory life drawings done in the studio in the conventional fashion. Jules Bastien-Lepage (1848-84) adopted the light palette and impulsive brushwork of Manet's young friends the Impressionists, and became the champion of the strain of 'official Naturalism' that was to take over the Salon in the years 1880-1900; much imitated outside France, this was the style that provoked vehement opposition from the Idealists and Symbolists.

238
Aimé-Jules Dalou
Le grand paysan, (Large Farmer), 1902.
Bronze. H. 197 ; W. 70 ; D. 68.
Purchased in 1905.

238

Dalou

Following the example of Courbet, Daumier and Zola, French sculpture determinedly reverted to the principles of 'Realism' - although in truth it had barely deviated from that course except under the influence of the academics. Vincenzo Vela (1820–91) in Italy and Constantin Meunier (1831-1905) in Belgium were among the innovators. They turned to their fellow men and women to find their subject matter, and dispensed with the window-dressing of historical, mythological or religious themes.

Jules Dalou (1838-1902) had played an active part in the 1870 Paris Commune and afterwards escaped to England with his family. It was from London that he submitted his design for the *Triomphe de la République (Triumph of the Republic)* in 1879, the year of the amnesty. Starting in 1889, Dalou worked on numerous studies for the never-completed *Monument au travail (Monument to Labour)* ; of the 150 realist studies of workers, only *Le grand paysan (Large Farmer)* was produced full-size.

Dalou's attention to everyday reality and his subtle modeling are particularly evident is more personal subjects like the small *Femme retirant son bas (Woman Removing her Stocking)*.

239

239
Aimé-Jules Dalou
*Femme retirant son bas
(Woman Removing her
Stocking)*.

Plaster. H. 34.8 ; W. 27 ; D. 21.2.
Purchased in 1934.

240
Aimé-Jules Dalou
*Masque de jeune fille
(Mask of Girl)*.

Terracotta.
H. 20.2 ; W. 13.3 ; D. 9.
Purchased in 1926.

240

Sculpture:
Aspects of Naturalism

Naturalism tended to focus on a highly specific category of subjects: life underground in the mines, dockers in the ports, peasants and the hardships of peasant life, and industry–the crucible of suffering, but also the foundation of the economic growth that was transforming the face of Europe. Manual work, reserved in the ancient societies for slaves, was now recognized as the nation's life-blood. In recognition of his new importance, the working man was given the vote.

Suddenly it was acceptable to study the distortions of his workworn body, his clothes and his way of life. The ideal of perfection embodied in Greek and Roman sculpture ceased to have any relevance: it was necessary to start afresh. The stylistic repertoire that had been developed over the years had

241
Constantin Meunier
Débardeur du port d'Anvers (Stevedore from the Port of Antwerp), 1890.
Bronze. H. 48.5 ; W. 23.5 ; D. 18.8.
Purchased in 1890.

242
Carl Milles
Mendiante (Beggar).
Bronze. H. 30.4 ; W. 17 ; D. 19.
Gift of Madame Nillet in memory of her husband, painter David Nillet, 1933.

241

242

243

243
Constantin Meunier
L'Industrie (Industry).

Bronze. H. 68 ; W. 91 ; D. 36.
Commissioned for the Musée du
Luxembourg in 1896, entered the
collection in 1897.
Fragment of a large relief
intended for the Monument to
Labour, on which Meunier
worked from 1885 till his death,
but did not manage to complete
during his lifetime.

become an obstacle to perception and free interpretation. Yet,
within a relatively short time, these innovations in turn ossified
into a system, became facile. The experimental was absorbed
once more into 'official' art. The success enjoyed by the style,
now respectable and accessible to all, is apparent in the proli-
feration of memorials that accompanied the expansion of urban
development. Fame itself was democratized, and vast numbers
of statues were erected of the great men of the day and of significant figures from the past (for example Dalou's *Lavoisier*, a
belated tribute now that the Republic needed scientists). These
furnish an incomparable source of material for historians - and
in some ways it is not inappropriate that they have themselves
in some instances been the victims of history. The bronzes, for
example, were melted down during the Occupation. Thus the
sketches displayed in the hall reserved for commemorative statues are of particular interest, because they are frequently the
sole record of vanished works.

246

247

244

244
Jean-Léon Gérôme
Sarah Bernhardt (1844-1923), circa 1895.

Polychrome marble.
H. 69 ; W. 41 ; D. 29.
Gérôme Bequest, 1904.

245
Jacques-Emile Blanche
Portrait of Marcel Proust,
1892.

Oil on canvas. H. 73.5 ;W. 60.5.
Donated in lieu of estate duties,
1989.

245

Parisian Life

246
Henri Gréber
*Jean-Léon Gérôme (painter
and sculptor, 1824-1904),*
1904.

Marble. H. 46.8 ; W. 15.2 ; D. 13.7.
Purchased in 1904.

247
Giovanni Boldini
*Comte Robert de
Montesquiou (writer,1855-
1921),* 1897.

Oil on canvas. H. 160 ; W. 82.5.
Gift of Henri Pinard on the sitter's
behalf, 1922.

248
Paul Troubetzkoy
Après le bal ou *Madame
Geltrude Anernheimer
(After the Ball,* or, *Madame
Geltrude Anernheimer),*
1898.

Bronze. H. 53 ; W. 66.8 ; D. 69.8.
Purchased in 1904.

249
Rembrandt Bugatti
*Jeune femme aux longues
manches (Young Woman
with Long Sleeves),*

Marble. H. 51 ; W. 20 ; D. 23.
Gift of Jean-Marie Desbordes,
1980.

Parisian and international high society presented a particularly dazzling, witty and elegant image during the period 1890-1900, as symbolized by the colossal *Parisienne* by Paul Moreau-Vauthier (1871-1936), placed over the entrance to the World Fair of 1900. A vital record of that society left by various portraits and busts of individuals; thus Henri Gréber (1854-1941), for example, executed excellent portraits of such fellow artists as Gérôme and Fremiet, while the Italian-born Russian sculptor Paul Troubetzkoy delighted in flowing, virtuoso statuettes of his society friends.

Three portraits nevertheless stand out for both their quality and their subjects. Gérôme's bust of *Sarah Bernhardt* (the most famous actress of her day, as well as being a painter and sculptor) is a striking combination of life-size bust and allegorical figures. Jean (Giovanni) Boldini (1842-1931), meanwhile, immortalized Count Robert de Montesquiou (aesthete, Symbolist writer, collector) in a free yet refined handling that conveys the count's haughtiness. In fact, it was Montesquiou's circle that inspired most of the characters in Proust's *Remembrance of Things Past,* the count himself serving as model for Baron de Charlus. Thanks to Jacques-Emile Blanche (1861–1942), we have a Whistler-like portrait of the dandyish Proust himself, the finest literary portraitist of Paris high society.

248

249

Symbolism

Symbolism was born of a reaction against official art 'effete and devoid of ideas', coupled with a desire to create a stylistic identity distinct from Impressionism. It was also the culmination of an urge to express abstractions by transposing them from one medium to another, in the Baude-lairian sense of 'correspondences' ('the symbol is the meta-phor, it is poetry itself,' wrote Verlaine), and, too, of an urge to appeal to the imagination ('My drawings inspire, they do not define,' wrote Redon).

From about 1890 the Symbolists exhibited regularly at the Salons of the Société Nationale des Beaux-Arts, where their dominant figures were Rodin, Puvis de Chavannes and Eugène Carrière (1849-1906), whose subtle brown monochromes are particularly well represented in the Musée d'Orsay. Symbolist works are typically composed of forms in movement, delibera-tely blurred or left incomplete; the subjects are many and various, with a decided leaning towards expression of the artist's inner turmoil and idealistic aspirations. Thus the ethe-real vision of Alphonse Osbert (1857–1939) could co-exist with the complex pictorial language and decadent details favoured by Edgard Maxence (1871–1954). Jean Carriès (1855-94), meanwhile, chose to dwell on death and the repose that it

250
Alexandre Séon
*Lamentation d'Orphée,
(Lament of Orpheus),* 1896.
Oil on canvas on wood.
H. 73 ; W. 116.
Gift of Fleury Grosmollard,
the artist's nephew and heir,
in 1917.

250

251
Paul Dardé
Douleur (Pain), 1913.

Gypsum. H. 49.5 ; W. 44 ; D. 38.2.
Purchased in 1919.

252
Edgard Maxence
*Femme à l'orchidée
(Woman with Orchid),*
1900.

Oil on wood. H. 0.575 ; W. 0.435.
Purchased in 1989.

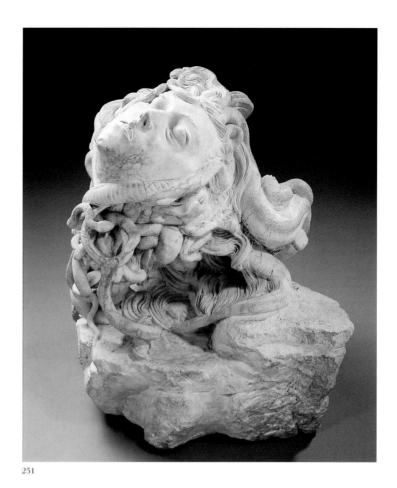

251

252

253

254

253
Fix-Masseau (Pierre-Félix Masseau)
Le Secret (The Secret), 1894.

Mahogany and ivory.
H. 76 ; W. 17.5 ; D. 18.
Purchased in 1894.

254
Alphonse Osbert
Vision, 1892.

Oil on canvas. H. 235 ; W. 138.
Gift in 1977 of Mlle Yolande
Osbert, the artist's daughter,
who enjoyed usufruct until 1986.

184

255

255
Jean Carriès
Charles I of England, 1887.
Bronze. H. 33 ; W. 62 ; D. 53.
Purchased in 1890.

256
Eugène Carrière
Paul Verlaine (poet, 1844-1896).
Oil on canvas.
H. 61 ; W. 51.
Purchased with help from
the Société des Amis du
Luxembourg, 1910.

brings, eschewing all attempt at realism in his head of *Charles I of England,* with the special elegance and softness of its flowing locks.

Sharing Carriès's sensitivity to materials, and attracted equally by sculpture and the creation of objets d'art, Pierre Roche (1855-1922), Jean Dampt (1854-1945) and Pierre Fix-Masseau (1869-1937) favoured unexpected subjects taken from medieval or Breton legend; they sought subtle, glimmering, often coloured effects reminiscent of Redon, Moreau or pastels by Lucien Lévy-Dhurmer (1865-1953).

256

Rodin

The Musée d'Orsay is particularly fortunate in having in its possession four large plaster casts on permanent loan from the Musée Rodin. It is thus possible to trace Rodin's development from *L'âge d'airain (The Bronze Age)*, with its naturalistic modelling, right through to the *Muse Whistler (Muse or Monument to Whistler)*, handled with such freedom that it amounts to little more than a number of loosely related elements, linked together by a piece of draped cloth dipped in plaster.

During the 1880s Rodin's major project was *La porte de l'Enfer (The Gate of Hell)* commissioned for the nation in 1880 and changed only in minor details after 1890, and also to a series of portrait busts. Both the *Gate of Hell* and the bust of *Dalou* reveal Rodin's admiration for the Italian Renaissance, the former being inspired by Dante's *Divine Comedy* Amid the tangle of bodies condemned by passion to the abyss, two principal episodes are represented: on the left, Paolo and Francesca locked in embrace (the origin of the famous *Baiser, The Kiss*), and on the right, the figures of Ugolino and his children (of which the exhibit in the Musée d'Orsay is a larger-scale copy). The *Gate of Hell* was too large to be worked in one piece of

258

260

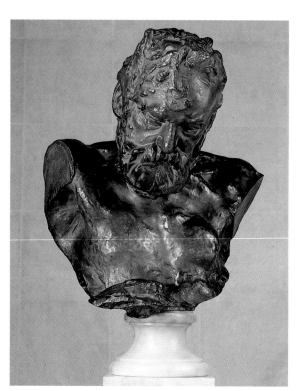

259

clay and was therefore modelled in sections, each of which exists as a separate sculpture: *Le Penseur (The Thinker)*, *Fugit Amor*, *Ombres (The Shades)*, etc.

Ultimately Rodin was to move increasingly in the direction of abstraction, as in *La pensée (Thought)* - which echoes another powerful image of human creativity, the bust of *Goethe* by Pierre Jean David d'Angers, situated in the entrance-hall of the museum - and, to outstanding effect, in his statue of *Balzac*. The change in his style can be measured by the progress from those early nude studies of visionary Realism, which become increasingly more simplified and distorted ('in my view, modern sculpture should exaggerate the forms to express mental attributes'), arriving finally at this pyramidal silhouette, the emphasis all on the large head. This almost abstract symbol of the novelist's powers aroused such a furore when it was shown to the public in 1898 that the commission was withdrawn. Today it is recognized as Rodin's most innovatory sculpture.

259
Auguste Rodin
Victor Hugo (1802–1885),
circa 1897.

Bronze. H. 70.6 ; W. 61.5 ; D. 56.8.
Purchased in 1906.

260
Auguste Rodin
L'Age d'airain (The Bronze Age).

Bronze. H. 178 ; W. 59 ; D. 61.5.
Purchased in 1880.

261
Auguste Rodin
Balzac, 1898.

Plaster. H. 275 ; W. 121 ; D. 132.
Permanent loan from the Musée Rodin, 1986. The photograph by Steichen was given to the Musée d'Orsay by A.S.D.A. in 1981.

A large area of the terraces on the first floor is devoted to
Auguste Rodin (1840-1917) and the group of young sculptors
who worked with him as assistants: Jules Desbois (1851–1935),
Antoine Bourdelle (1861–1929), Lucien Schnegg (1864-1909),
and Camille Claudel (1864-1943), whose masterpiece *L'âge mûr
(Maturity)*, inspired by the ending of her relationship with
Rodin, is shown together with the latter's sculptures.

262
Camille Claudel
*L'Age mûr (Age of
Maturity)*, 1894-1903.
Bronze. H. 114 ; W. 163 ; D. 72.
Purchased in 1982.

Foreign Painting and Sculpture

Until the very end of the nineteenth century, few serious efforts were made to secure works by foreign painters for the contemporary collection of the Musée du Luxembourg (one of the exceptions being Oswald Achenbach, during the Second Empire). If non-French painters were represented, it was usually because they were resident in France. No one thought to take advantage of the unique opportunity presented by the World Fairs, with their international art exhibitions, and when the idea surfaced in 1900 it was already too late to do much about it.

In 1915, Edmund Davis donated his collection of English painting, and an annexe was opened at the Jeu de Paume, in 1922, specifically for foreign works. Even so, the museum had no major painting by Sir Edward Burne-Jones (1833-98) until that deficiency was remedied recently by the acquisition of *The Wheel of Fortune* - which was, in fact, one of the artist's own favourite works: Puvis de Chavannes had tried unsuccessfully to have it included in one of the first Salons of the Société Nationale des Beaux-Arts, of which he was then President. Burne-Jones, associated with the second 'romantic' phase of Pre-Raphaelitism, reveals in this picture a debt to Michelangelo, Mantegna and Botticelli, whose works he studied in the course

263

264
Sir Edward Burne-Jones
The Wheel of Fortune, 1877-
1883.

Oil on canvas. H. 200 ; W. 100.
Purchased in 1980.

265
Arnold Böcklin
*La Chasse de Diane (Diana
the Huntress),* 1896.

Oil on canvas. H. 100 ; W. 200.
Purchased in 1977.

264

265

266

of his last trips to Italy, in 1871 and 1873, and who were to have a profound influence on the paintings of his maturity.

The Swiss painter Arnold Bocklin (1827-1901) avoided France but stayed in Italy on several occasions. Elements of Symbolism begin to appear in his work from around 1870 onwards. His landscapes, whether calm or stormy, have a peculiar atmospheric quality that suggests the forces of nature at work; the mythological figures he introduces are no more than a confirmation of the stated theme. *La chasse de Diane (Diana the Huntress)* is a reworking of a theme treated thirty years before, and still betrays its original classical influences. Italian inspiration and the influence of Poussin can also be detected in *Siesta* by Hans Thoma ((1839–1924), another Germanic artist. Here, however, mythology is abandon in favour of a bucolic idyll.

George Hendrik Breitner (1857–1923) was one of the most well-known Dutch artists of his day, and was considered important by Van Gogh (the two men often worked together in the early 1880s). Breitner's *Clair de Lune (Moonlight)*, its troubling atmosphere tinged with Romanticism, is remarkable above all for its spare forms.

Painting in the 1880s and 1890s was largely dominated by different schools of Realism, often variants and extensions of movements in French painting such as Impressionism and Neo-Impressionism (Divisionism). In the last ten years of the century there was a trend towards Symbolism, variously interpreted in the different countries.

La dame en détresse (The Lady in Distress) of 1882 belongs to the early period of the Belgian painter James Ensor (1860-1949).

267

He was influenced initially by Impressionism, but in the 1880s moved on to more domestic themes, following the *intimiste* paintings of artists like Bonnard and Vuillard. Later still, his canvases reflected an interest in the unconscious, becoming increasingly Symbolist in character, representing masks and grotesque figures that are in a direct line of descent from Hieronymus Bosch.

In Italy around 1892-95, Giuseppe Pellizza da Volpedo (1868-1907) adopted a technique derived from French Neo-Impressionism, as did Vittore Grubicy di Drago, Angelo Morbelli and - outstandingly - Giovanni Segantini. Pellizza drew extensively on social and humanitarian themes, but a work such as *Fleur brisée (Broken Blossom)*, c.1896-1902, demonstrates that he also understood the vocabulary of Symbolism.

267
Winslow Homer
Summer Night, 1890.

Oil on canvas. H. 76.7 ; W. 102.
Purchased in 1900.

268
Léon Frédéric
Les Ages de l'ouvrier (The Ages of the Working Man),
circa 1895-1897.

Oil on canvas. Triptych.
Central panel: H. 163 ; W. 187.
Right panel: H. 163 ; W. 94.5 ;
Left panel: H. 163 ; W. 94.5.
Purchased in 1901.

268

269

269
George Hendrik Breitner
Clair de lune (Moonlight),
circa 1887-1889.

Oil on canvas. H. 101 ; W. 71.
Purchased in 1989.

270
Giuseppe Pellizza da
Volpedo
*Fleur brisée (Broken
Blossom)*, circa 1896-1902.

Oil on canvas. H. 79.5 ; W. 107.
Purchased in 1910.

Of a different order altogether is the Symbolism of the Belgian painter Léon Frédéric (1896-1940). His great triptych *Les ages de l'ouvrier (The Ages of the Working Man)* is a celebration of manual labour in a style verging almost on Hyper-Realism, belonging to the same vein of social Symbolism as the contemporary works of his compatriots Constantin Meunier and Eugène Laermans.

One of the dominant figures in American painting was the Bostonian Winslow Homer (1836-1910), who discovered Impressionism when he visited Paris. His love of the sea is reflected in his *Summer Night*, a mysterious and resonant painting of great evocative power.

270

271
Piet Mondrian
*Le départ pour la pêche
(Setting Off to Fish),*
circa 1898-1900.

Pastel, watercolour and charcoal.
H. 62 ; W. 100.
Purchased in 1987.

The early career of Mondrian, one
of the pioneers of abstraction, was
heavily indebted to 19th-century
Dutch pictorial tradition. In this
painting however, despite its
conventional subject, Mondrian's
linear construction of space and
limited palette are harbingers of
future experimentation.

272
Giovanni Segantini
*Le porteur de fagots
(Carrying Firewood),* 1899.

Pastel and charcoal.
H. 36.5 ; W. 56.
Purchased in 1979.

272

273

273
Franz von Stuck
*Ludwig van Beethoven
(1770-1827)*, 1900.

Painted plaster.
H. 48 ; W. 48 ; D. 14.
Gift of the Société des Amis
d'Orsay, 1992.

274
Medardo Rosso
Ecce puer ou *Impression
d'enfant (Ecce Puer*, or,
Impression of a Child).

Bronze. H. 44 ; W. 37 ; D. 27.
Gift of Francesco Rosso,
the artist's son, 1928.

In sculpture, Max Klinger and Franz von Stuck (whose work only entered the collections in 1990 and 1992), are among the best representatives of German symbolism: the red eyes of Klinger's *Cassandra*, and the mask and colouring of von Stuck's *Beethoven*, underscore those works' striking impact. Pieces by Augustus Saint-Gaudens and Medardo Rosso are examples of the rather infrequent purchases of foreign sculpture by the French nation, in 1899 and 1928 respectively.

274

275
Max Klinger
Cassandre (Cassandra).
Bronze. H. 59 ; W. 32 ; D. 35.
Purchased in 1990.

276
Augustus Saint-Gaudens
Amor Caritas, 1885.
Bronze. H. 264 ; W. 127 ; D. 30.
Purchased in 1899.

Drawing and Watercolour

277
Jan Toorop
*Le Désir et l'Assouvissement
(Desire and Fulfillment),*
1893.

Pastel on beige paper.
H. 76 ; W. 90. Purchased in 1976.

The Nabis were enthusiastic practitioners of all the graphic arts - prints, posters, book illustrations, etc. - and between them produced a vast quantity of drawings, those by Bonnard being probably the finest and most attractive. His wide-ranging imagination is evident both in rapid sketches and more finished pastels and watercolours. Théophile Steinlen (1859-1923), in a more down-to-earth spirit, presents us with a vivid picture of his times. Cappiello' character-sketches reflect the revival of poster art, also embodied by Jules Chéret (1836-1932) and Toulouse-Lautrec. The Symbolists too, like Gustave Moreau, were draughtsmen; the drawings of Lévy-Dhurmer or Carlos Schwabe, for example,

277

278
Lucien Lévy-Dhurmer
La Femme à la médaille ou
*Mystère (Woman with
Medal,* or, *Mystery),* 1896.

Pastel and gold highlights
on cardboard-backed paper.
H. 35 ; W. 54.
Gift of M. and Mme Zagorowsky,
1972.

278

are of particular appeal to contemporary taste. As in a similar vein, although different in mood, are the works of the Italian Segantini, the Belgian Leon Spilliaert (1881-1946), and the Dutchman Jan Toorop (1858-1928). Major decorative schemes for stained glass, furniture, glass and jewelry – devised by the likes of Grasset, Gallé, Lalique and Mucha – illustrate the extraordinary phenomenon of Art Nouveau.

279
Eugène Grasset
Le Travail par l'Industrie et le Commerce enrichit l'Humanité (Industry and Trade Enrich Humanity), 1900.

Design for a stained-glass window commissioned by the Paris Chamber of Commerce.

Watercolour and gouache on paper.
H. 65 ; W. 99. Gift of the Société des Amis d'Orsay, 1993.

279

280

280
Pierre Bonnard
Design for an Interior
(detail).

Pen and watercolour.
H. 50.5 ; W. 53.8.
Gift of Alice et Marguerite
Bowers, 1984.

281
Eugène Emmanuel Viollet-
le-Duc
*Furnishing fabric, design
for* Histoire d'une Maison,
circa 1870-1873.

Watercolour. H. 19.6 ; W. 11.2.
Purchased in 1980.

282
George Mann Niedecken
*Proposed decoration of the
living room of the Irving
House* (Decatur, Illinois), built
by F. L. Wright in 1909-1910.

Pen and black ink, watercolour
on canvas. H. 71 ; W. 66.
Purchased in 1985.

281

282

283

Léopold Van Strydonck
"La lutte du bien et du mal" (Struggle Between Good and Evil), elephant tusk with stand, 1897.

Ivory, bronze. H. 76 ; W. 70 ; D. 35. Purchased in 1989.

284
Auguste Delaherche
Vase, 1889.

Glazed stoneware. H. 38.
Gift of Mme René Bureau, 1993.

285
Clément Massier
Ewer, circa 1893-94.

Faïence with metallic lustre. H. 85.
Gift of Mme René Bureau, 1993.

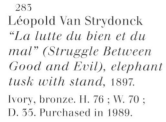

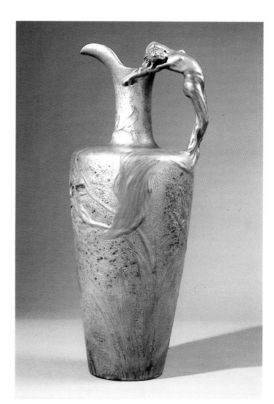

284

285

202

Art Nouveau

286
Ernest Chaplet
Vase, 1900.

Hard-paste porcelain, high-fired decoration. H. 45 ; Diam. 19.9. Purchased in 1900.

287
Jean Carriès
Cache-pot, 1892.

Glazed stoneware, gold highlights. H. 16 ; Diam. 16.8. Purchased in 1892.

The last third of the nineteenth century saw a revival in architecture and the decorative arts. Art Nouveau was born out of a determination to reject the conventional and create an entirely new stylistic vocabulary. It was initially referred to as 'modern art' or 'the modern style'; only in 1890 did the term 'Art Nouveau' come into use, capitalized to mark its status as a distinctive style.

The movement achieved its major successes between 1890 and about 1905, although this varied a little from one art to another, as they reacted to external influences at different times. Thus the lessons of Japan and the Far East were absorbed first by the ceramicists, whose work perhaps reached its peak in the period between the two World Fairs of 1878 and 1889; certainly that was the first real intimation of the blossoming of Art Nouveau yet to come. Powerful and vigorous ceramics were produced at that time by Ernest Chaplet (1835-1909), Auguste Delaherche (1857-1940) and the great Jean Carriès (1855-94), who abandoned sculpture in favour of pottery.

286

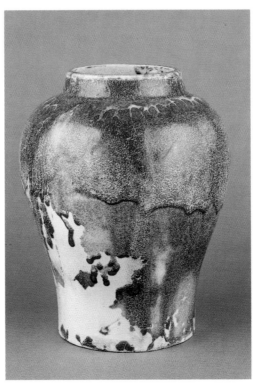

287

288

288
Rupert Carabin
Bookcase, 1890.

Walnut and wrought iron.
H. 290 ; W. 215 ; D. 83.
Purchased in 1983.
This was the first of twenty
pieces of furniture design by
Carabin.

Following pages:
289
Alexandre Charpentier
Dining room, 1901.

Mahogany and gilded bronze;
fountain and tiling of glazed
stoneware by Alexandre Bigot.
H. 346 ; W. 105.5 ; D. 621.
Purchased in 1977.
Installed in the Champrosay villa
of banker Adrien Bénard.

After 1905 Art Nouveau became derivative, although it continued as a force up to the outbreak of the First World War: its themes and motifs dwindled into mediocre repetitions of once-original designs, and were overtaken by an emergent rationalism that rejected the exuberance of its flowing decorative curves.

Although a short-lived phenomenon, Art Nouveau is not easy to pin down and describe, as it was by no means a homogeneous entity. There are, however, a number of fundamental principles that draw the different threads together.

First of these is the belief in the Unity of Art - the notion that art is one, even in its many and various manifestations one notable consequence of which, in France, was the abolition of the distinction between the 'major' and the 'minor' arts, so that in 1891 the annual Salon of the Société Nationale des Beaux-Arts included examples from the applied arts as well as painting and sculpture. In fact the part played by sculptors in the evolution of Art Nouveau design was quite significant, and a number of them turned their attention to domestic items. The pewter vessels produced by Jean Baffier (1851-1920) are robust, powerful pieces; Jules Desbois (1851-1935) made silver and pewter plates and flasks with incised designs of female nudes with flowing tresses. Jean Dampt (1854-1945), Alexandre Charpentier (1856-1909) - for a time members of an association called, significantly, 'Art dans Tout' ('Art in Everything') - and Robert Carabin (1862-1932) went beyond the production of everyday objects to produce complete domestic interiors.

The role played by painters was perhaps less decisive, although in 1884 Victor Prouvé (1858-1943) provided the glass-maker Emile Gallé with a number of designs based on the human figure to be used as motifs in glass engravings; and in 1895 the dealer Siegfried Bing (1838–1905) exhibited in his newly opened gallery, itself called 'L'Art Nouveau', a famous series of stained-glass windows by L. C. Tiffany (1848-1933) based on sketches by Toulouse-Lautrec and the Nabis.

290

Another principle of Art Nouveau, constantly reiterated, relates to the form of objects: this held that construction must always be related to use, and form and decoration must arise out of the material used. As a theory this was functional in the extreme, but the results in practice were often the reverse of what was intended.

In fact, the aesthetic vocabularies adopted by individual artists diverged widely, despite common ideals, a shared desire to reject models from the past (freeing themselves from what Gallé called 'archaeological poison' - although here once again the vociferous verbal protestations against official art were often tempered in the actual work itself), and a universally held belief in the possibility of creating new forms and decorations for a modern age. Indeed, even their artistic philosophies differed, depending on their personal inclination or on the historical or cultural influences that affected the places where they lived and worked (Brussels, Paris, Nancy, Vienna, Glasgow, etc.). Looked at in this light, it is hardly surprising that the work produced in these various centres was so diverse.

To the members of the School of Nancy, in eastern France, nature itself was the only admissible source of inspiration. Although the School was formally constituted only in 1901, it had in effect been active over the previous thirty years, dominated by the figure of Emile Gallé (1846 1904). Roger Marx (1859-1913), another citizen of Nancy, described him as '*homo triplex*', referring to his prowess as a ceramicist, glassmaker

291

292

291
René Lalique
Neck chain and pendant,
circa 1903-1905.

Gold, enamel, brilliant-cut
diamonds and aquamarine.
H. 6.9 ; W. 5.7 ; D. 0.8.
Purchased in 1983.

292
René Lalique
Scent bottle, circa 1900-1902.

Mold-blown glass (lost-wax
method), chased gold.
H. 10.5. Purchased in 1988.

293
Eugène Feuillâtre
Bonbonnière, 1904.

Crystal, enamel and silver.
H. 8.3 ; Diam. 14.5.
Purchased in 1904.

293

294

and cabinet-maker. Always experimenting and looking for new ideas, Gallé was responsible for numerous technical advances and decorative innovations, interpreting models from nature with seemingly inexhaustible imagination and an unfailing aesthetic sense. He never deployed his prodigious technique gratuitously: it is always subordinated to a superb creative intelligence, uniting form and content in a harmonious whole. His emphasis on nature influenced other artists from the same region, such as Eugène Vallin (1856-1922) and Louis Majorelle (1859-1926), the two great cabinet-makers of the School of Nancy. Encouraged by him, they developed a distinctive style of their own, abandoning their earlier pastiches of the medieval or eighteenth-century manner. The furniture they produced is outstanding in its finish and the quality of materials employed, and demonstrates a remarkable ability to use decoration as an integral element of an overall design.

294
Emile Gallé
Liseron d'octobre (Autumn Convulvulus), vase, 1891.
Two-layer crystal, inlay, chased decoration, base in cut, chased cristal. H. 18.8 ; Diam. 9.8.
Purchased in 1892.
Engraved with a line from Verlaine which might be translated as "How you bow, autumn convulvulus, over my melancholy."

295

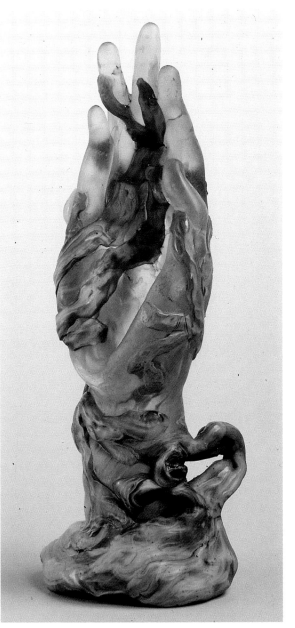

295

Emile Gallé
La limnée des étangs (Pond Snail), vase in the shape of a freshwater snail (Lymnaea), designed in 1884.

Clear glass, partly burnished, inlays, intaglios, opaque enamels. H. 31.6 ; Diam. 12.4.
Purchased in 1985.

The motif of putti playing on snails was supplied by Victor Prouvé.

296

Emile Gallé
La Main aux algues et aux coquillages (Hand with Seaweed and Shells), 1904.

Chased crystal with inlay and appliqués. H. 33.4 ; W. 13.4.
Anonymous gift, 1990.

296

297
Emile André, architect,
Eugène Vallin, joiner and
cabinet-maker, **Jacques
Gruber**, master glazer
Double door.

Mahogany, "Tiffany" and
opalescent glass, gilded bronze.
H. 198 ; W. 182 ; D. 6.5.
Purchased in 1983.
From the fitting room of the
François Vaxelaire store built
in Nancy in 1901.

299
Louis Majorelle
"Waterlily" bedside table,
circa 1905.

Mahogany, acacia, marquetry,
gilded bronze. H. 110 ; W. 55 ;
D. 45. Purchased in 1980.

298
Emile Gallé
"Dragonfly" showcase,
1904.
Ironwood, pin oak, mahogany,
rosewood, mother-of-pearl,
bronze and gemstones.
H. 234 ; W. 134 ; D. 64.5.
Purchased in 1982.
Commissioned by Paris
magistrate Henry Hirsch, this
was Gallé's last piece of
furniture.

One of the Art Nouveau ideals was to unite form and decoration in an organic unity. The theoretical basis for this idea rested largely on the Naturalistic principles put forward by Viollet-le-Duc, which were based on his studies of medieval architecture: that line should be free and untrammelled, that structure and decoration should be one and the same, the major function of ornamentation being to illustrate structure. In Brussels and Paris, the architects Victor Horta (1861-1947) and Hector Guimard (1867-1942) developed their own distinctive interpretations, and they eliminated anything that might disrupt the unity of the concept, designing even the door-knobs and handles, the espagnolettes for the windows and the bathroom tiles. Guimard referred with some pride to the 'Guimard style', and indeed it is impressive how the vocabulary is carried through over the whole range of materials, wood, cast and wrought iron, copper, glass, etc.: evidence of a desire for artistic integrity. After the turn of the century, the fashion for the characteristic features of Art Nouveau, asymmetry and 'whiplash'

300

300
Hector Guimard
Garden vase and pedestal,
circa 1905-1907

Cast iron. H. 135.5 ; W. 59 ; D. 45.
One of the 56 pieces designed by Guimard and cast by the Saint-Dizier foundries, donated by Mme de Menil in 1981.

301
Hector Guimard
Armchair, 1903.

Pear, original covering of tooled, chased leather. H. 106 ; W. 76 ; D. 56. From Castel Val in Chaponval, built 1902-1903. Purchased in 1989.

302
Hector Guimard
Room fitting in the form of a fireplace, circa 1897-1898.

Jarrah and linden wood, chased copper. H. 302 ; W. 179 ; D. 29. Purchased in 1979.
From a residence renovated by Guimard at Les Gévrils (Loiret), when he was working on the Castel Béranger.

301

303
Gustave Serrurier-Bovy
Bed, circa 1898-1899.

Mahogany, decorative details in
copper, original panels of
embroidered, painted silk.
H. 279 ; W. 211 ; D. 240.
Purchased in 1984 with the rest
of the bedroom furnishings
including two wardrobes, a
dresser, and full-length swivel
mirror.

303

304

304
Henry Van de Velde
Desk, designed in 1898-1899.

Oak, gilded bronze, copper,
leather. H. 128 ; W. 268 ; D. 122.
Purchased in 1987 thanks to
Crédit Lyonnais Bank.

305
Peter Behrens
Armchair, circa 1902.

Stained oak. H. 105 ; W. 62 ;
D. 52.5. Purchased in 1987.

curves, was on the wane: the decoration and furnishings of the Hôtel Aubecq (1902-24) are more restrained and severe than those of the Hôtel Solvay, and the patterns designed by Guimard and cast by the Saint-Dizier foundry (1903-7) are more harmonious and regular than those used in the Castel Béranger. In the work of Gustave Serrurier-Bovy (1858–1910), who regarded himself as operating in the populist traditions of the Arts and Crafts Movement, curves are used purely as linking elements and not to emphasize structure. Unlike Horta and Guimard, he used metal decoration as surface relief on his items of furniture.

305

306

306
Richard Riemerschmid
Chair, designed in 1902.

Oak, straw-bottomed.
H. 82 ; W. 43 ; D. 48.
Purchased in 1989. Produced by
Dresdener Werkstätten für
Handwerkskunst.

307
Heinrich Vogeler
"Spaziergang" tapestry,
designed in 1899.

Wool and cotton. H. 60 ; W. 100.
Purchased in 1987. Woven at
Scherrebecker Kunstwebschule.

307

308

308
Carlo Bugatti
Chair, 1902.

Wood sheathed in painted, gilded
parchment, and copper.
H. 0.97 ; W. 0.37 ; D. 0.53.
Purchased in 1992.

309
Henri de Toulouse-Lautrec
and Louis Comfort Tiffany
*Au nouveau cirque, Papa
Chrysanthème (At the New
Circus, Papa
Chrysanthemum) stained
glass,* 1894-1895.

Marbled, printed and flashed
glass, cabochons. H. 120 ; W. 85.
Gift of Henry Dauberville on
behalf of his children, Béatrice
and Guy-Patrice Dauberville,
1979.

309

Glasgow, Vienna, Chicago

In the early 1890s Art Nouveau spread throughout Europe and the United States. In 1894, Otto Wagner (1841–1918) designed Vienna's first example of 'modern' architecture, the Karlsplatz metropolitan railway station. In the same year, in Chicago, Louis Sullivan (1856-1924) completed the Stock Exchange building, its strongly stated decorative theme emerging naturally from the structure.

The World Fairs provided an international forum for artists, and various publications were started in the wake of the exhibitions - the most important of which were held in Chicago in 1893, Brussels in 1897, Paris in 1900, Turin in 1902, and Saint Louis in 1904. The annual exhibitions of the avant-garde (such as the 'Libre Esthétique' in Brussels and the 'Secession' in Vienna) provided another meeting-place for artists and encouraged the exchange of ideas. Lavishly illustrated art periodicals ensured that news of recent developments reached a wide audience. Thus Charles Rennie Mackintosh (1868-1928) was better known for his decorative work, which was given publicity in the art magazines and exhibited abroad (notably in Vienna in 1900), than for his major buildings in Glasgow.

Yet the success of the international 'modern style' of Art Nouveau was short-lived. The interchange of ideas between the architects of Glasgow and Vienna led in turn to a more radical reappraisal of form, and a move in the direction of geometrical abstraction. When, in 1903, Josef Hoffmann (1870-1956) and Koloman Moser (1868-1918) founded the Wiener Werkstätte - a complex of studios for industrial artists, modelled on the contemporary English craft guilds - they were far more

310
Koloman Moser
Music case, circa 1904.

Leaded and black-varnished oak, carved and gilded wood, chased silver-plate, Babitt metal, glass. H. 199.5 ; W. 200.5 ; D. 65.5. Purchased in 1988. Produced by the Wiener Werkstätte.

311
Otto Wagner
Armchair, designed in 1900.

Tinted and varnished beech, brass, modern covering. H. 79 ; W. 66 ; D. 60. Purchased in 1986.

311

310

312

312
Koloman Moser
Inkwell and tray, 1905.

Silver, glass.
H. 7 ; W. 22.6 ; D. 15.
Purchased in 1986. Executed
by goldsmiths from Wiener
Werkstätte.

314

315

313
Josef Hoffmann
Armchair with adjustable back, circa 1905.

Beech and plywood, mahagony stain, iron. H. 110 ; W. 62 ; D. 82. Purchased in 1986. Manufactured by J. & J. Kohn.

314
Adolf Loos
Café chair.

Varnished beech, cane seat. H. 87 ; W. 42.5 ; D. 51. Purchased in 1981. Model designed by Loos in 1898 pour the Museum Café in Vienna, and manufactured by J. & J. Kohn.

315
Thonet Bros.
Chair No. 51.

Ebonized ash, cane seat. H. 91.3 ; W. 41.5 ; D. 53. Purchased in 1984. Model probably designed by August Thonet for the Astoria Hotel in New York in 1888.

313

concerned to appeal to an élite of aesthetes than to produce articles at a modest price aimed at the mass market.

It was not until the turn of the century that the Viennese architects began to take an interest in bentwood furniture, although it had in fact been pioneered in Vienna by Michael Thonet and mass-produced there for thirty years. The prototypes of furniture devised at this period by Adolf Loos, Siegel, Josef Hoffmann and Otto Wagner are among the finest the twentieth century has produced.

Loos (1870-1933) worked outside the Secession, whose doctrinaire attitudes he criticized in polemical articles. An admirer of the New World, he believed passionately in the need for a functionalism that corresponded to the requirements of modern life.

Over the same period, in the United States, Frank Lloyd Wright (1869–1959) designed his Prairie Houses, superb examples of the integration of architecture with its Environment. Anticipating the European avant-garde by several years, he successfully developed a style of pure abstraction, exemplified by his use of coloured glass in the Coonley house (1908).

316

316
Frank Lloyd Wright
Chair.

Oak and leather.
H. 125 ; W. 45 ; D. 51.
Purchased in 1982. From the
Isabel Roberts' house (River
Forest, Illinois) built by Wright
in 1908.

317
Charles Rennie Mackintosh
Dressing-table and mirror.

Painted wood, ebony and mother-
of-pearl, silver-plated bronze,
glass.
H. 179.6 ; W. 101.6 ; D. 45.7.
Gift of Michel David-Weill, 1985.
From the house of Catherine
Cranston (Hous'hill, Glasgow),
renovated by Mackintosh in 1904.

317

318
Aristide Maillol
La Méditerranée (The Mediterranean),
1923-1929.

Marble.
H. 110.5 ; W. 117.5 ; D. 68.5.
The maquette was exhibited at
the Salon d'Automne, Paris, 1905.
Marble commissioned by the
nation, 1923.

Maillol,
Bourdelle, Bernard

319

'The complete work of art will be that... in which the most contrary, the most apparently contradictory qualities - strength and gentleness, discipline and grace, logic and abandon, precision and poetry - will sit together with such ease that they seem natural and not in the least surprising. Which means that the first thing that must be renounced is the pleasure of amazing one's contemporaries.' This new aesthetic doctrine was formulated by the writer André Gide, as a reaction both against Rodin and against academic art.

Although the undulating lines of the *Danseuse (Dancer)* by Aristide Maillol (1861-1944) still bore some resemblance to those beloved of Symbolism and later Art Nouveau, it was nevertheless Maillol who produced the first and most brilliant manifestation of what has come to be known as the Stylistic Renewal (*retour au style*): the sculpture *La Méditerranée (The Mediterranean)*, exhibited at the Salon of 1905. Static and uncommunicative, it must have stood out against Rodin's figures, described by Gide as 'quivering, anxious, gesticulating, full of noisy pathos'. Gide went on: 'Monsieur Maillol's large seated woman... is beautiful, she means nothing... I think we have to go back a long way to find such a complete disregard for any other concern except beauty.'

Maillol chooses a single viewpoint and simplifies his composition: there are no tensed limbs, no symmetries, but strictly defined and distinct elements that fill up their allotted space. If the frame were removed from one of his reliefs, the spectator would mentally replace it, obedient to the dictates of the composition. This same desire for simplification is apparent in the treatment of the surface, which is of untroubled regularity and smoothness.

320

320
Aristide Maillol
Le Désir (Desire), 1905-1907.
Lead. H. 120 ; W. 115 ; D. 25.
Allocated by the Office des Biens
Privés, 1951.

321
Joseph Bernard
*Effort vers la nature
(Toward Nature),* circa
1906-1907.
Stone, direct carving.
H. 32 ; W. 29 ; D. 31.5.
Gift of Jean Bernard, 1980.

321

322

322
Emile-Antoine Bourdelle
*Héraklès archer (Hercules
the Archer)*, 1909.
Bronze. H. 248 ; W. 247 ; D. 123.
Purchased in 1924.

In 1900, putting behind him the Romantic indulgences of his youth, Antoine Bourdelle (1861-1929) turned to Greek models for inspiration. He then executed *Tête d'Apollon (Head of Apollo)*, in 1900-9, *Pénélope (Penelope)*, in 1905-8, and *Héraklès archer (Hercules the Archer)*, a superb example of his compositional skill and ability to produce rhythmic variations of stillness and tension. Charles Morice wrote of it: 'The extraordinary exaggerated stance of the archer poised in space... that human form which seems to surge forward even in immobility, that incisive and accurate modelling, so full and vibrant; it is one of the most prodigious efforts of contemporary art.'

Whereas Gauguin and Lacombe - and Maillol in his early years - had carved almost exclusively in wood, Joseph Bernard (1866-1931) adopted the practice of direct carving in stone. His *Effort vers la nature (Towards Nature)* suggests, both by its title and its massive, primitive appearance, a desire for close harmony between form and matter; it was the prelude to works carved directly out of huge blocks of stone, in the manner that was to be adopted by Henry Moore, Amedeo Modigliani, Jacob Epstein and Constantin Brancusi. Bernard's figures are more supple and rhythmic than Maillol's, with a spirituality reflecting the artist's own mysticism. A particularly fine example is the *Porteuse d'eau (Water Carrier)* of 1912.

323
Emile-Antoine Bourdelle
Tête d'Apollon (Head of Apollo), 1900.
Bronze. H. 67.4 ; W. 27.2 ; D. 25.3.
Donated in lieu of estate duties, 1989.

324
François Pompon
Hippopotamus.
Bronze. H. 14 ; W. 6.5 ; D. 22.5.
Pompon Bequest, 1933.

324

After 1900

325
Pierre Bonnard
L'après-midi bourgeoise ou
La famille Terrasse
(A Bourgeois Afternoon, or,
The Terrasse Family), 1900.

Oil on canvas. H. 139 ; W. 212.
Donated in lieu of estate duties,
1988.

The Nabis did not hold together as a coherent group much beyond 1900, when the individual members began to develop in their distinctive ways, while still maintaining their friendship. Bonnard, after reverting to a more realistic manner, notably in his portraits, then became absorbed in exploring the possibilities of colour in a series of magnificent nudes and still-lifes. Remaining largely outside the major movements of the early twentieth century - Fauvism, Cubism and Abstraction - he continued his investigations of the pictorial space, as in *En barque (In the Boat)*, which looks down over its subject and makes use of the widest possible visual field. This vast composition was the prelude to sumptuous panoramas of landscapes at Vernon and Le Cannet.

325

326

Bonnard, Vuillard, Denis and Roussel never lost the taste for decoration acquired in their early Nabi years. Vuillard produced decorative ensembles for Claude Anet and Henri Bernstein, and decorated the villa at Villers-sur-Mer owned by the Bernheims, Paris picture dealers. Otherwise he continued to paint domestic subjects and also numerous portraits: those in the Musée d'Orsay collection include likenesses of many of the notable personalities of the day, the Comtesse Jean de Polignac and Jeanne Lanvin among them.

In vast dynamic compositions in brilliant colours, Roussel explored mythological themes such as *L'enlèvement des filles de Leucippe (The Abduction of the Daughters of Leucippus)*. His pastels too are peopled with nymphs and fauns.

A number of the former Nabis were reunited in 1912-13 when they worked together on the decoration of the Théâtre des Champs-Elysées, built by the Perret brothers. The cupola was painted by Maurice Denis, while Vuillard and Roussel respectively undertook the decoration of the foyer and drop-curtain of the adjoining Comédie des Champs-Elysées.

326
Pierre Bonnard
La loge (The Theatre Box),
1908.

Oil on canvas. H. 91 ; W. 120.
Donated in lieu of estate duties,
1989.

230

327

327
Pierre Bonnard
En Barque (In the Boat),
1907.

Oil on canvas. H. 278 ; W. 301.
Purchased in 1946.

328

329
Edouard Vuillard
Deux femmes brodant sous une véranda (Two Women Embroidering on a Verandah), one of seven decorative panels executed for the Bernheims' villa, Bois-Lurette, at Villers-sur-Mer, 1913.

Oil on canvas. H. 201 ; W. 113.5. Gift of Henry Dauberville on behalf of his children Béatrice and Guy-Patrice Dauberville, 1979.

328
Ker-Xavier Roussel
L'Enlèvement des filles de Leucippe (Abduction of the Daughters of Leucippus), 1911.

Oil on canvas. H. 430 ; W. 240. Purchased in 1935.

329

With Symbolism and Art Nouveau at their peak, the World Fair held in Paris in 1900 demonstrated a poverty of creative inspiration in Western painting as a whole - and that in spite of the continued presence of masters of the Impressionist generation such as Monet, Cézanne and Renoir, and also Gauguin and Bonnard. The transition between the centuries was not to be a smooth progression but a brutal wrench, the banner of modernity being taken up by a largely new generation of younger artists. Yet, clearly, twentieth-century art had roots in the past: Gustav Klimt (1862-1918), Ferdinand Hodler (1853-1918) and Edvard Munch (1863-1944), for example, were the direct precursors of German Expressionism, but at the same time they had close links with Symbolism.

In France, new departures in architecture by Perret and Sauvage, and by Maillol in sculpture, were matched by two new movements in painting: these were Fauvism, which burst onto the scene at the Salon d'Automne of 1905, and Cubism, which may be said to have begun with Picasso's *Demoiselles d'Avignon* (1907; The Museum of Modern Art, New York). Cubism, its indebtedness to Cézanne notwithstanding, was a movement that reached out to the future, very much a twentieth-century phenomenon. Fauvism, on the other hand, lasted barely a few years and was really no more than the exploration of one facet of the Post-Impressionist aesthetic, the exploitation of colour. It is for this reason that the Musée d'Orsay shows a number of Fauve paintings, among them *Luxe, calme et volupté* by Matisse, which shows a direct link with Divisionism. Henri Matisse (1869-1954), together with his friends from student days in Gustave Moreau's studio, Georges Rouault (1871-1958) and Albert Marquet (1875-1947), was one of the leaders of the Fauve movement, with which Georges Braque (1882–1963) was for a time associated. Their colleagues André Derain (1880-1954) and Maurice de Vlaminck (1876-1958) - the so-called School of Chatou - were, like the German Expressionists, the inheritors of the tradition of Van Gogh.

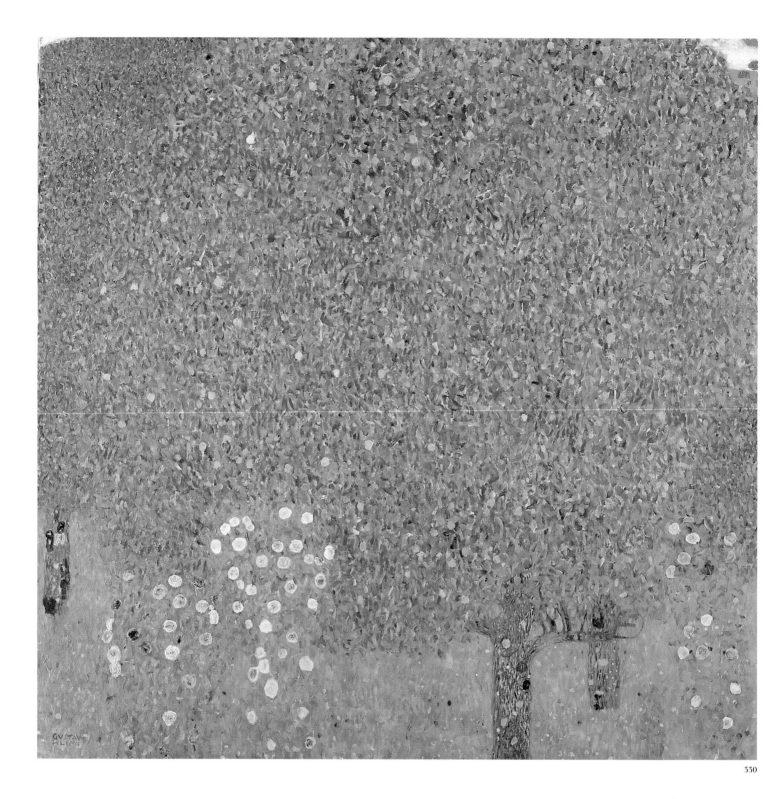

330
Gustav Klimt
*Rosiers sous les arbres
(Roses under Trees)*, circa
1905.

Oil on canvas. H. 110 ; W. 110.
Purchased in 1980.

331
Edvard Munch
*Nuit d'été à Aasgaarstrand
(Summer Night,
Aasgaarstrand),* circa 1904.

Oil on canvas. H. 99 ; W. 103.5.
Purchased in 1986.

332
Ferdinand Hodler
Schynige Platte, landscape
near Berne, Switzerland, 1909.

Oil on canvas. H. 67.5 ; W. 90.5.
Purchased in 1987.

331

332

333

333
André Derain
Charing Cross Bridge, circa
1906.

Oil on canvas. H. 81 ; W. 100.
Max and Rosy Kaganovitch
Bequest, 1973.

334

334
Henri Matisse
Luxe, calme et volupté
(Luxuriance, Peace,
Pleasure), 1904.
Oil on canvas. H. 98.5 ; W. 118.5.
Donated in lieu of estate duties,
1982.

*From the Publications
Department directed by
Anne de Margerie*

Editor Sylvie Messinger

*English translation:
Jane Brenton (1987),
Deke Dusinberre (revised
edition, 1995).*

Production Jacques Venelli

Layout Scarabée

*Photoengraving by
Sept Offset, Champigny-sur-
Marne*

Paper, Job 150 g

*Printed in june 1995, by
de Snoeck Ducaju & Zoon,
in Belgium.*

Dépot légal : june 1995
I.S.B.N. : 2-7118-3282-1
GA 20 3282